THE BELOVED:

ST. MUNGO, FOUNDER OF GLASGOW

Writer, editor, and illustrator since his Oxford days, Reginald Hale has been engaged in making as well as writing history. During World War II, he served in Europe with the U.S. Air Force, winning the Bronze Star Medal, and he also edited the U.S. 8th Air Force magazine.

After the war, he travelled widely as editor of *New World News*, a global magazine with editions in 24 languages. When he was 50, his war disabilities forced him to retire, and he and his wife settled in Ottawa, Canada.

In recent years, his field of study has been the lives of the Celtic saints who so greatly influenced the history of the British and Irish races. His book *The Magnificent Gael* tells the story of St. Columba of Iona. Lord Macleod, founder of the Iona Community, wrote of this book: ''No other biography. . . has caught, in such concise compass and with such warmth of appreciation, the true image of the saint. . . . Columba speaks to our day.''

REGINALD HALE, F.S.A. Scot., is a Fellow of the Celtic Chair, University of Ottawa.

To Milton & Margaret —

THE BELOVED

ST · MUNGO ·
Founder of Glasgow

Reginald B. Hale

Reginald B · Hale F·S·A·Scot·

University of Ottawa Press
Ottawa • London • Paris

© University of Ottawa Press, 1989
Printed and bound in Canada
ISBN 0-7766-0260-8 (casebound)
ISBN 0-7766-0227-6 (paperbound)

Canadian Cataloguing in Publication Data

Hale, Reginald B., 1911-
The Beloved: St. Mungo, founder of Glasgow

Includes index.
ISBN 0-7766-0260-8 (casebound)
ISBN 0-7766-0227-6 (paperbound)

1. Kentigern, Saint, 518?-603. 2. Christian
saints — Scotland — Biography. I. Title.

BR1720.M86H34 1989 270.2'092'4 C89-090018-3

UNIVERSITÉ D'OTTAWA UNIVERSITY OF OTTAWA

Typeset in Caxton Book by
Nancy Poirier Typesetting Limited, Ottawa

To Archie Hutchison
of Glasgow

Historian, poet and man of God,
who first inspired my interest
in St. Mungo

Contents

Foreword

I know of no one more suitable and better informed to write on the subject of St. Mungo, or Kentigern as he was also called, than Reginald Hale, whose excellent work on St. Columba is so well esteemed and was of such value to me in my research for my novel, *Columba*. Mungo was a renowned missionary to Strathclyde and Wales in the sixth century at approximately the same time as Columba was bringing the Gospel to Dalriada and Alba, the two parts of what is now Scotland. The names and fame of these two great men have resounded down the ages.

Reginald Hale's scholarship, enthusiasm and sheer devotion to his subject ensure that this book will not only fill a major gap in our knowledge and appreciation of this vital period in our Christian story, and of a very remarkable character, but also make fascinating reading into the bargain.

Nigel Tranter, OBE
Aberlady,
Scotland

Principal Characters

AIDAN
  Sent from Iona as bishop to Oswald's kingdom

AIDAN MACGABHRAN
  King of the Scots, Domelch's husband

ALCHFRID
  King of Cumbria, famed for his learning

ARTHUR
  Battle-leader of Britain in the early sixth century

ASAPH
  Abbot of Llanelwy, Wales

AUGUSTINE
  First Archbishop of Canterbury

BRIGET OF KILDARE
  Irish saint

BRUDE MACMAELCHON
  High King of the Picts

CADOC
  Famous Welsh teacher

CADWALLON LIU
  King of Tegeingl, Wales

COELIUS
  Last Roman army commander of Britain

COLUMCILLE
  Irish prince who founded Iona

COMGALL OF BANGOR
  Abbot of Bangor, comrade of Columcille

CYNFARCH
  Urien's father, King of Reged

DENIOL
  Founder of Bangor Fawr monastery, Wales

DIARMID MACCERBAILL
  High King of Tara

DOMELCH
  Brude's daughter, consort of Aidan MacGabhran

EDWIN AND ETHELBERGA (TATA)
  King and Queen of Northumbria

ELIFER
  Gwendoleu's younger brother

GARTNAIT MACDOMELCH
  High King of the Picts

GILDAS
  Fiery Welsh writer

GREGORY
  Abbot of St. Andrew's, Rome; Pope, 590–604

GWENDOLEU
  Pagan usurper of Reged

ILTUD
  Famous Welsh teacher

KENNETH OF ACHABO
  Irish abbot who accompanied Columcille to meet
  King Brude

KENTIGERN OR MUNGO
  Bishop and founder of Glasgow

LOTH
  King of Dunpelder in the Lothians; Mungo's grandfather

LUGBE MOCU BLAI
  Columcille's personal secretary

MAELGWN
  Powerful King of Gwynedd, Wales; called ''The Island Dragon''

MERLIN
  Arch Druid

MOLUAG
  Missionary founder of Lismore

MONENNA
  Irish missionary nun who taught Tannoc

MORCANT BULC
  Pagan king who drove Mungo into exile

MORDRED
  Loth's son; led rebellion against Arthur

OSWALD AND OSWY
  Ethelfrith's two sons, educated at Iona; both Kings of Northumbria

OWEN
  Prince of Reged, father of Mungo

PATRICK
  Patron Saint of Ireland

PAULINUS AND RHUN
  Bishops who baptized the English in the north

PEADA
  Son and heir of Penda, King of Mercia

PELAGIUS II
  Pope whom Mungo went to meet in Rome

PENDA
  Embittered King of Mercia

REINMELTH
  Princess of Cumbria; wife of King Oswy of Northumbria

RHUN
  Son of Maelgwn; led the Long March

RYDDERCH
  King of Strathclyde, Scotland

TANNOC
  Daughter of Loth, mother of Mungo

URIEN
  Military leader of the Christian cause

Preface

Glasgow is Scotland's largest city, rightly renowned worldwide because events that happened there have affected every part of the world.

It was while walking on Glasgow Green in 1763 that James Watt thought out the idea of the steam engine. "I had not gone further than the Golf House," he said, "when the whole thing was arranged clearly in my mind." In Glasgow, therefore, was born the Industrial Revolution with its factories, railways and steamships — the Clyde-built steamers that carried Scots by the million to Canada and Australia and ferried the "toiling masses of Europe" to settle the New World.

Fittingly the founder and patron of Glasgow was a pioneer, who in a darkened world faced frightening odds to bring back the light of Christianity to Scotland and the neighbouring countries. Glasgow remembers him affectionately by his nickname — Mungo, the Beloved. The city's coat of arms displays a robin, a bell and a salmon with a ring in its mouth, each referring solely to Mungo.

The astonishing fact is that Mungo was born around 525 AD. He was a Roman Briton and he lived when the great Arthur ruled Britain.

Here is a story worth exploring.

The sixth century AD is called "the lost century." It is the despair of scholars. In the breakdown of the Roman Empire, the keeping of records ceased, and the very

Britain and Ireland in the Sixth Century

method of dating years was lost. Yet it was in this dark period that certain men lived who profoundly influenced history. Mungo was one of them. No one wrote anything about him until 1181, five centuries after he died. Yet his story was passed down by his people in oral traditions.

There are three reasons why it is important to study ''the lost century'':

1. In this period, the blood stock of the British people was decided — mainly English but with a large intermix of Celtic blood, larger than is often realized.

2. The common language of the British people was decided — English but with a rich intermix of Celtic, Norse, French and Latin, making it an inclusive language, concise and expressive.

3. The faith of the people was decided. The British became Christian.

If these decisions had been made differently, the British, Canadians, Americans, Australians and many more would be unrecognizable as such today. We would not think, act or speak as we do. Our customs, laws, schooling and ideals would all be different. Mungo of Glasgow played a prominent role in the third decision — the faith of the people — and therefore a study of his life is relevant.

The noted historian William Skene wrote in 1886 in his *Celtic Scotland*: ''As Columcille was the founder of the Christian Church among the Picts in the North of Scotland, so Mungo was the great agent of the revolution that again Christianized Cumbria, South Scotland and Northern Britain.''

My interest in "the lost century" began in 1970 when I became fascinated by the life of Columcille of Iona — Ireland's greatest son, founding father of the Scottish nation, and surely the most attractive of our people's ancestors!

A legacy made it possible for my wife and me to travel through Ireland and Scotland, visiting the places associated with the saint. In Donegal at Loch Gartan we stood by the "birthing stone" on which he was born in 521; we strolled by the Boyne at Clonard where he was educated, wandered through Tara of the Kings and through the yellow gorse that covers the fateful battlefield of Culdremne. In Dublin I had the rare privilege of holding in my hand Ireland's oldest book, the *Cathach*, a psalter penned by Columcille's own hand. In Scotland we entered the cave at Loch Killisport where Columcille and his men sheltered when they arrived from Ireland. And we walked up the pebble beach at Iona where his "Island Soldiers" came ashore in 563.

How can one trace the footsteps of such a man through the scenes of his life without being drawn into a richer understanding and a sense of fellowship with him?

In 1976 I published a book about Columcille called *The Magnificent Gael* which has sold steadily for a dozen years. Now is the time to trace the steps of Mungo, Columcille's friend and colleague.

*   *   *

Our search first led us to an eminent scholar at a famous university. "Can you tell us what you know about

Mungo?'' we asked. He replied frankly, ''We are not sure that St. Mungo ever existed.'' In Oxford we visited Blackwell's bookshop in Broad Street. Oxford men grow up believing that Blackwell's can find any book on any subject. ''Can you check for all texts about Mungo?'' we asked. Obligingly their hi-tech computers began to clatter, but the read-out showed nothing on record.

After a few such experiences we realized that Mungo could not be traced by the usual method of library research. We must develop a method more like military intelligence. As in the case of Columcille, we must explore the locations that tradition associates with Mungo's life.

Traprain Law seemed the place to begin. This rugged rock rises 700 feet above sea level 20 miles east of Edinburgh. Here in the sixth century AD was the town and fortress of Dunpelder, ruled by a Roman Briton, King Loth, from whom the Lothians take their name. Loth was Mungo's grandfather.

Today Traprain Law is used to train rock-climbers who dream of scaling Everest. Yet, if we were to understand the story of King Loth and his grandson, it seemed necessary that we climb this crag. Aged 75 and partly disabled, I was a poor candidate for rock-climbing, but perhaps there was some way up. In the nearby town of Haddington lived my wartime friend Captain Mike Barrett. We had served on the staff of the same General. I asked his advice. His neighbour George knew two Eagle Scouts, trained climbers, whom he recruited. So we three veterans — all old enough to know better — and our wives who were going along to keep an eye on us, set off for the summit guided by the Eagle Scouts. Halfway up we passed over the ruined town wall of Dunpelder. At the summit a vast view opened before us: the Firth of Forth and the Isle of May and, on the horizon of the North Sea, ships 30 miles away were clearly visible. At our feet the rocky crag fell sheer and awesome 300 feet straight down.

To us Dunpelder ceased to be just a dot on a map or a note in a history book. To us now it is a vivid, unforgettable memory. Thus we started to track the footsteps of Mungo.

Acknowledgements

I have had generous helpers in this task and wish especially to thank Margaret Halliday of the staff of St. Mungo's Cathedral, Glasgow, for her help in so many matters. My thanks go also to the Bishop of St. Asaph who sent me a rich store of documentation about the years when Mungo worked in North Wales. Dr. Neville Haile of Colwyn Bay took me exploring on the Degannwy peninsula to see the stronghold of the great King Maelgwn. In Cumbria we enjoyed the hospitality of Carol Sarsfield-Hall at Keswick. She showed us Druid circles and ancient wells where Mungo preached and baptized. Dr. Lewis MacKay of Wimbledon and Dr. George Mintsioulis of Ottawa tackled the challenge of diagnosing the cause of King Maelgwn's blindness and its cure.

I feel especially grateful to Gwen McLellan of Ottawa who not only can read my writing but can correctly spell Gaelic words and even Welsh ones. My thanks go also to the Court of Lord Lyon and to Glasgow District Council for permission to reproduce the shield of the city arms on the cover, to the gifted heraldic artist Karen Bailey who has painted them so beautifully and to her sister, Barbara, who drew the maps, making it easier for readers to walk in Mungo's footsteps.

I am deeply grateful to Father Leonard Boyle, OP, Prefect of the Vatican Library in Rome, for his kind encouragement and advice. It has been a blessing to walk in the footsteps of Mungo and come to love this splendid British saint to whom our countries owe so much.

MUNGO'S WORLD

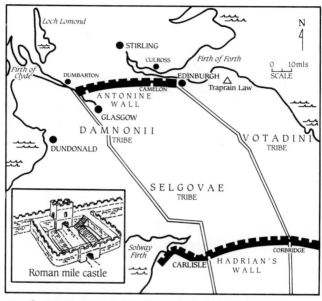

North Britain, guarded by the Antonine Wall and Hadrian's Wall.

Chapter one

The world into which Mungo was born had been shaken loose from its foundations. Rome, which for centuries had given a solid base of law, order and civilization, was crumbling. Overrun by barbarian hordes from the east, its fabric gave way.

Britain had been ruled by Rome for over 400 years, nearly as long as the white man has been in America. But in 410 AD the legions were withdrawn from Britain and the islanders had to face the future on their own. They had to ward off invasions of Picts from the north, Irish from the west and the Anglo-Saxons from the east. Had the Britons been united, they could have guarded their shores, but they were split into two hostile parties: the Pagan Party (also called the Native Party) which clung to the old Celtic-Druidic lore and learning; and the Roman Party which upheld Roman culture and the Christian religion. Britain's chief ruler, Vortigern, leader of the Pagan Party, tried to strengthen his hand by hiring Saxon mercenaries. He began to lose control of the situation and attempted to promote a peace conference with the Roman Party. However, the Saxons by treachery broke in on the peace delegates and massacred all the Roman Party leaders, leaving Vortigern a helpless puppet in the Saxons' hands.

These were terrible years for Britain but, at the end of the century, from the ranks of the Roman Party arose an inspired battle-leader, Arthur. On a dozen battlefields he shattered the power of the Picts and the Irish and then, in 516, he crushed the Anglo-Saxon army at Mount Badon. His victories won for Britain 20 years of peace. These years lingered in the memory of the Britons as ''the Golden Years of Peace'' and it was during these years that Mungo was born.

Many Britons still thought of themselves as Romans. This was particularly true of those who lived on the frontier near the two Roman walls which defended the north. The Antonine Wall stretches for 57 miles from the River Forth to the Clyde. This was a ''checkline'' to disorganize an enemy attack. Supporting it to the south was the stone-built Hadrian's Wall, stretching 70 miles from the Tyne to the Solway, and this was the ''stopline'' where an invasion had to be halted.

People who live on a frontier maintain their identity more fiercely than those who live in peaceful areas. Many North Britons were descended from generations of Roman soldiers, who came out year by year from all over the Empire to serve on the two Roman walls. Theirs was a rather isolated world, military and conservative, an environment of camps and trumpet calls, of discipline and following the Eagle standard, of the Games and the baths. After 30 years of service the veterans retired, receiving as their coveted reward Roman citizenship for themselves and their children. Few ever returned to their homelands, which were no longer home for them. They married local girls and settled near the familiar walls, forming an élite leadership of the society of the north.

As the Roman Empire's troubles multiplied, its lines of supply broke down. The paymaster's convoy with the pay for the troops had always arrived as regularly as Spring. When it ceased to come, the army commander in York sent urgent messages to the Roman cities in the prosperous south of Britain. But the citizens of the south had little incentive to tax themselves to maintain soldiers far away in the north. Finally the army commander in York had no alternative but to tell his troop commanders to fend for themselves. So the troops were sent out "foraging." "Looting" was what the country-folk called it. Little by little, each garrison commander became an independent petty-king. An unplanned chaotic patchwork of minor kingdoms sprang up across the land over a period of two or three generations.

The last Dux Britannarum ("Army Commander-in-Chief") at York was Coelius, "Old King Cole" of the nursery rhyme. As each of his subordinate officers broke away, he conferred on him a portion of his authority. These officers became known as "Sons of Coelius." They were of course not his natural sons but were staff officers of his "military family." This has led to considerable confusion among those who try to deduce royal lines of descent for the Coelian "Kings."

Around and between the Roman walls lived three British tribes, all of which were ruled by kings descended from one of these Roman staff officers. The Votadini lived along the North Sea coast from Berwick to the Lothians and up the River Forth as far as Stirling. Their capital was at Dunpelder near the site of Edinburgh. They had always been devoutly loyal to Rome and had therefore been granted the special privilege of raising their own cohort (regiment) to march behind their Red Dragon standard. West of them in the gloomy forest of the Selkirks lived the Selgovae, and they were pagan and hostile to Rome. In the valley of the Clyde were the Damnonii, kinsmen of the Dumnonii who lived in Devon and Cornwall. Both branches of this tribe were traditionally allies of Rome. The capital of the Damnonii was the crag of Dumbarton on the River Clyde — "the fort of the Britons." Their cohort bore a Green Dragon standard.

Throughout the known world, the frontiers of the Roman Empire had fallen, militarily and politically. The Vandals had sacked Rome itself, yet in this remote corner of Britain around the walls the people felt that in some way they still stood on guard, defending civilization against barbarian attack.

Although Rome's frontiers were in ruin, there was a frontier that still ran through people's hearts. In much of Europe men clung to the values and ideas of Rome, proud of its splendid achievements and mourning for its lost glory. And there was another frontier too — the Christian frontier. Rome's frontier was defensive, exclusive. The Christian frontier was inclusive, throwing wide the door to all who wished to share in the vision of a new life and a new world. These two frontiers are perfectly illustrated in the well-known story of the Roman Briton Patrick, Patron Saint of Ireland.

Chapter two

The open frontier of the Christian faith works in surprising ways. At the beginning of the fifth century AD, Patrick was 16 years old, his home probably at Kilpatrick near Glasgow on the Clyde. His grandfather was a Christian priest and his father was a deacon and civic official. Then one day the Irish slave raiders came. In his book, *De Excidio Britanniae (The Destruction of Britain)*, Gildas has described such a raid: ''With hairy villainous faces, the Irish swarm out of their curraghs like maggots.'' With hundreds of others Patrick was rounded up, fettered and driven aboard the ships. The helpless rage and humiliation of the slave market was followed by the aching loneliness of work as a herdsman on the hills of Slemish in Ulster.

Alone on the hills he found strength in prayer. At 22, he had the courage to escape and reach Gaul. He was trained and ordained as a priest and returned to Britain, probably with the Apostolic Mission of Bishop Germanus in 420. Patrick's mind was gripped by a conviction that he must return to Ireland and win for Christ the people who had enslaved him. In 432 he sailed across and landed at Downpatrick in Ulster to begin his incredible mission. So daring and so abiding was his impact on Ireland that it is still the greatest single event in Irish history.

What can explain its effect? Ireland was never part of the Roman Empire and, when Patrick faced the High King at Tara, no legions tramped behind him. He brought within himself an irresistible idea and, in his own life, proof of its truth. Irish society was built on loyalty to family. To them, that was the highest moral virtue. No man stood alone but was part of his ''derbfine'' — the true family, all the descendants of his great-grandfather.

Each was duty-bound to resist and revenge any affront to the family honour. So the whole of Irish society was interlocked in an unending cycle of feuds of revenge. The Irish understood that Patrick had every right to hate and seek revenge against them. Instead he had come back of his own free will to forgive them! It defied belief, yet he was walking proof of the words of Jesus: "Forgive us our sins as we forgive those who sin against us." And the warm, generous Irish hearts opened.

In most legends about Patrick the theme of forgiveness is central. The *Senchas Mor* — the Great Record of the Laws of Ireland — states: "Retaliation prevailed in Ireland before Patrick, and Patrick brought forgiveness with him. So now, no one is executed for his crimes so long as he pays *eric* — the blood fine." The dynamic of forgiveness freed the Irish spirit from the endless tit-for-tat of the blood feud. It explains the brilliant explosion of learning and creative art, "the Golden Age," when Ireland became "the land of saints and scholars."

It should be noted how large a part women played in the spreading of Patrick's message. Of all the women of Ireland, the glory of Briget of Kildare shines brightest. Next to Patrick she is acclaimed as the founder of the Irish Church. One of the thousands of girls inspired by Briget was Monenna of Newry, who was to play a very significant part in Mungo's story. Her real name was "Edana" to which was added the affectionate prefix "Mo." Monenna founded a convent on her own tribal land but she soon found it was a mistake to be so close to home that aunts and cousins could drop in at all hours, involving the nuns in family squabbles. She consulted Briget of Kildare and her advice to Monenna was to move

further away to the north. Monenna was always search-
ing for better systems of training and, when she heard
of the famous monastery at Whithorn in Britain, she sent
her most gifted nun to learn their rules and practices.
Her contact with Whithorn drew her into extending her
work to northern Britain.

This was the period of "Arthur's peace." Arthur
was building a chain of defended towns to protect the
Britons from invaders. In the north, they were placed at
Dundonald, Dumbarton, Stirling, Dunedin and Dunpelder.
Monenna decided to establish a church or convent at each
of these places to match Arthur's strategy. At the summit
of the rock where Edinburgh Castle now stands, she built
a small oratory for herself. The hill became known as
"Edana's Hill," later called Dunedin and long afterwards
Edinburgh.

Chapter three

It takes imagination to visualize what the "town" of Dunpelder was like at that time, high on the great rock shoulder of Traprain Law, 20 miles east of Edinburgh. It is the peak of a huge rock, towering 700 feet above sea level; look-outs posted on its crest could watch any ship approaching the Firth of Forth from 30 miles out to sea.

The man who commanded this strategic post was King Loth. He was descended from the last Roman praefectus appointed by the Emperor Valentinian (d. 392) to command this part of North Britain. He was typical of the petty-rulers who proliferated after the time of Coelius.

In spite of having assumed a royal title, Loth still thought of himself as a Roman officer. He wore the broad ornamental officer's belt and the red cape of a praefectus and regarded himself as guardian of the imperial frontier against the barbarians. Oral traditions collected by Jocelyn of Furness, a twelfth-century Norman monk, tell us that Loth was "Rex semi-paganus" and that "he had a daughter under a step-mother. The daughter's name was Tannoc."

In his royal hall high on the cliff, more barrack than palace, there were few comforts of civilization — some silver goblets and Mediterranean pottery retrieved perhaps from a pirate ship, a tapestry or two, gifts from friends down south — yet it was enough to impress the locals. And there was entertainment, for even petty-kings had bards to sing to the harp the praises of their employer — clever young men who were politically inclined to the Pagan Party and its Druidic aristocratic beliefs, and who served as the royal advisors.

If Monenna wished to establish a convent near Dunpelder, she had to win permission of this rather unfriendly king, but she was a hard woman to refuse. She pointed out the advantages of teaching the girls at Dunpelder the skills of reading, of music and embroidery and of speaking and writing good Latin. In the end, King Loth consented and even allowed his daughter Tannoc to become a student at the convent.

The convent where Tannoc went to school was some distance from the town wall of Dunpelder. Around the convent was a rath — a mound and ditch. At its centre was a wooden church made of planed planks under a thatched roof. There was one large thatched building for a refectory and kitchen, and around it a cluster of huts for the nuns. Instruction was given in the open air or in the church.

What were the children taught at the convent? Probably much the same as St. Finnian taught his pupils in Ireland at the same time, and St. David in Wales and St. Samson in Brittany. The day began with a tinkling bell calling them to Lauds in the chapel and with the singing of psalms. They learned by heart the Lord's Prayer, the Nicene Creed, the Ave and many psalms. Reading and penmanship took up the morning; then some worked on embroidery and others in the kitchen garden. Raising food for the community was essential. Gardening also taught them to cooperate with nature, seeing the unfolding plan of God. They learned to observe and respect wild creatures, birds and animals, to treat them as friends and neighbours. This love and understanding of birds and beasts is a marked feature of all the Celtic Christians.

What was it that attracted these young folk to such an ordered life? The world around them was dark and full of fear, the strong preying on the weak. Power and wealth were life's only aims, force the means of attaining them. The economics of plunder ruled the world in the wreck of the Roman Empire. Close behind the plunderers trotted their jackals — slavery, massacre and plague. The unseen world too was ruled by pitiless spirits. Folk guarded themselves as best they could with charms and votive sacrifices but the haunting question always remained unanswered: was there any meaning or purpose to life?

People like Monenna offered an answer: the meaning and purpose of life is God. God is a father, close enough to speak to you if you will listen. He will speak to the ear of your heart. Tannoc the motherless child responded joyously. The story that gripped her imagination most was that of Mary, the Virgin Mother of Jesus. Here was her model for life — ''the pure in heart shall see God.'' This promise became her life's purpose and meaning.

It was a short walk from King Loth's hall to his daughter's convent. Yet they were untold worlds apart.

Chapter four

When Tannoc was 15 years old, there was high excitement up at the king's hall upon the rock. An important
visitor was coming. He was Prince Owen, the grandson
of King Cynfarch of Reged, the richest of the northern
kingdoms. Its capital at Carlisle controlled the western
end of Hadrian's Wall. It was the only place north of York
that could truly be called a city. It still had its city walls,
its public buildings surrounding the forum, many handsome villas and baths that still worked. Citizens of Carlisle
still felt like Romans. At the cavalry barracks at Stanwix
the successors of the famed Petronia regiment stabled
their horses. They were a formidable fighting force.

Prince Owen would some day rule this kingdom. He
was about 17 years old and had just "taken arms"
according to the Celtic custom when a boy became a warrior. He was on a semi-diplomatic mission to visit neighbouring kings, to make friends and possibly seek out some
well-born young lady worthy to be a queen.

Loth saw the possibilities of an alliance between his
small east-coast realm and the wealthy west-coast Reged.
It set his ambition afire. Messengers hurried down to the
convent to bring Tannoc up to the hall and get her dressed
in her finest clothes. She was given instructions that she
was to make herself pleasant to the prince. When they
met, he was charmed and asked her father for permission
to propose marriage to her. But when he asked her, her
answer was as crushing to his princely pride as to her
father's dreams of glory. She replied firmly, "I am already
promised to a King far greater than you will ever be."

Tannoc was very young and absorbed in her new-
found vision of holiness. She did not give a thought to
Prince Owen as a person. Had she done so she might

have drawn him to share her faith. Instead her crushing reply made the prince feel spurned and he hurriedly left for home.

News that Prince Owen had left drove King Loth into a frenzy, as he saw the chance of a valuable alliance vanishing. His royal will was rarely crossed. In rage he stormed at his daughter but failed to move her. So he had a swineherd brought to the hall and gave his daughter a choice: ''Either you marry Prince Owen or I shall give you as a bondservant to this swineherd.'' Still unflinching, Tannoc was led away by the herdsman.

It must have been a silent journey out to the pig farm on the Lammermuir. Only then did the herdsman speak. ''My Lady, I and all my family are Christian,'' he said, ''and we shall do all in our power to protect you.'' But there were other ears interested to learn Tannoc's whereabouts. Druidic courtiers at the hall had no wish to see Christianity flourish. They followed Prince Owen and told him where he could find Tannoc alone in the forest herding the pigs.

He caught her alone. Her refusal, he said, had robbed him of his dignity, so in return he would rob her of her virginity. Afterwards he went on his journey back to Carlisle. One could wish to pass over Tannoc's agony in silence but to do so would rob meaning from the story of St. Mungo, for it was his mother's lonely struggle that forged his own invincible courage.

Shocked, disgusted, furious, alone in the woods, Tannoc felt all the rage and humiliation that every raped woman has felt down the centuries and still feels today. Abandoned by her father, scorned by her own privileged class, she was alone and friendless. Was this the end of all the bright hopes she had had at the convent? With all her heart she had tried to choose God's way. What would become of her now? And, most dreadful thought — had God Himself abandoned her? None can guess how long she suffered through this bitter crisis. The Christian women at the farm surely offered her support, especially during the shock of realizing that she was pregnant. Did she rebel against this uninvited life inside her? Perhaps she then realized that the baby was as much a victim as she was herself, with no one to turn to for help, and she poured out the full passion of her love to cherish him. In so doing, she found her own destiny.

The months wore on, but there were spying eyes and whispering tongues and when her time was near her father was told of her condition. Self-righteous in his rage, he ordered the soldiers to arrest her and bring her in. She faced him in the hall calmly and without anger. By customary law unwed girls who became pregnant were doomed to be stoned to death. Her father passed sentence on her but not a soldier would pick up a stone. "It is unfitting," they said, "that anyone should throw a stone at one of the royal family." So, instead, a cart was produced and in it Tannoc was pulled up to the summit of Traprain Law. Oral tradition recalls that, as the cart was pushed over the edge, she cried out "Mary!"

The cliff is a sheer drop of 300 feet. At the bottom had gathered a group of her women friends from the convent. When the rubble and dust had settled, to their amazement they saw Tannoc bruised and bleeding, but alive. The cart may have acted as a toboggan, protecting her in the slide down the cliff.

TANNOC'S TERRIBLE JOURNEY

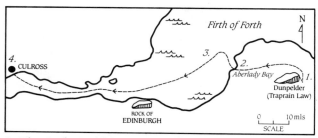

1. King Loth's soldiers took Princess Tannoc in a cart to the top of the precipice of Traprain Law and pushed her over the 300-foot drop. She survived.
2. The soldiers then took her six miles north to Aberlady Bay on the Forth and set her adrift in a coracle.
3. When the tide turned the coracle was driven westward up river all night, about 30 miles.
4. At dawn it was beached on the river bank at Culross. There her son Mungo was born.

They had little time to praise God for the miracle. Mounted soldiers arrived and took Tannoc away. This time she was "to be put on the sea in a boat of one hide, without sail or paddle." She was carried seven miles north to Aberlady Bay, a place where fishermen cleaned and gutted their catch. The area stank of rotten fish and sea-gulls screamed overhead. She was placed in a wicker cora-cle, scarcely larger than a basket, and towed out towards the Isle of May. There she was set adrift on the ebbing tide as the sun began to sink.

* * *

Even then her father's fury had not cooled. Convinced that it was the swineherd who was responsible for his daughter's condition, he gathered his war-band and set out to the Lammermuir countryside. But warning moved faster than he did. The Christian farmers scattered their womenfolk and cattle to safe places and armed themselves. It is not easy to run down a countryman in his own terrain and somewhere in the forest King Loth blundered into an ambush and a well-aimed spear put an end to the angry life of Loth of the Lothians.

Chapter five

Out in the Firth of Forth the coracle rocked on the slack tide. The evening sun went down, leaving a primrose yellow streak across the western skyline. Tannoc could see the jagged profile of Mount Edana silhouetted against it. But her teacher Monenna was far away in Pict country. The girl was aching and weary after a brutal, bruising day and she curled up on the floor of the coracle, glad just to lie still. Out of the wind she felt less cold. She noted the boat's idle motion had changed to a steady pressure pushing towards the west. The tide had turned.

And she was not alone. She felt two hearts beating within her. A strange peace enfolded her and she sang softly, "My soul doth magnify . . . He hath regarded the lowliness of His handmaiden . . . from henceforth all generations shall call me blessed." Then she slept. It was dark when she was awakened by the first birth pangs. She sensed rather than saw the high banks of the river. The coracle was moving erratically, pushed by crosscurrents towards the shore. It snagged a jagged rock. Carefully Tannoc worked her way to the bank, wading through oozy black mud until at last she found firm ground on shore. The flood tide and east wind had brought her 30 miles up river during the night. There was a pile of brushwood on the beach that offered a little shelter from the dawn wind. She lay down behind it and was startled when out of the brush flew a red star, then another and another until a tongue of flame sprang up. Someone had made a campfire here the night before and the east wind was blowing the ashes into flame. She lay in the warmth of the fire and here her baby was born. He was an illegitimate child of a homeless refugee, but he was her son. She had already chosen a name for him which tells much of this young woman's courage and sense of humour.

"Kentigern" she called him. In her Britonic Welsh tongue
it meant "big chief."

In the dawn one of the shepherds who had made the
campfire the evening before returned to the shore and
found the mother and child. At once he raced back to
his village nearby. It was a Christian community and he
roused the village priest who hurried to the river. Gently
he lifted the boy from Tannoc's arms. "Mynn cu," he
said, "my beloved." And Mungo he has been ever since.

The good priest and his flock adopted them and made
a home for them in their village of Culross. To the priest
and community the arrival of Tannoc and her son seemed
almost like their own personal Nativity. The girl's survival
after so many murderous attempts on her life could only
be a divine miracle. The priest realized that there was
danger in harbouring a royal fugitive, although King
Loth's death removed much of the danger. Culross chose
to close ranks around mother and child, to defend them
as their own. The priest would find in Tannoc a precious
reinforcement in his parish work. She was the most educated person in the village, literate, trained in the sacra-
ments and the services of the Church. She was almost
a fully trained nun, able to teach the young and comfort
the old.

But Mungo was her first care. Tannoc herself had
grown up in what was considered a patrician Roman
household and she would pass on to her son the manners
and habits of her background. She belonged to a generation that still cherished the healthy and pleasant Roman
practice of the daily hot bath and taught her son to enjoy
this cleanliness. He practised it to the end of his long life.

Another lesson he learned from Tannoc was the sensitivity of all Celtic Christians to the wild creatures of nature. Long walks with his mother by the river and in the forests were his college. He learned the names of flowers and their seasons, the feeding and mating habits of birds and beasts and how to win the confidence of the furred and feathered creatures. No one who has a beloved family dog can doubt an animal's ability to love, understand and communicate in wordless language with humans. It is not only domestic animals that have this gift, but men rarely allow a relationship of trust to develop with wild creatures. Mungo learned to understand animals, fish and birds with his heart. All through his life this gift came to light, as it does in the first story of his boyhood.

At Culross one day some robins were pecking on the ground for scraps. Village boys, as boys will, started throwing stones at them. One bird was hit and fell to the ground. The boys ran away. Mungo ran too, but he ran to the fallen bird. Picking it up he smoothed and caressed its feathers and prayed over it. After a little while it revived and flew away. Perhaps it was only stunned. The villagers called it a miracle and so it was that a small boy should want to help a fallen bird in trouble. Yet it was instinctive for Mungo, given the training he had received from his mother. That robin flew right into Glasgow's city coat of arms where now it proudly perches on the top of the oak tree.

In many accounts of St. Mungo's birth and boyhood, the good priest of Culross is called St. Serf who founded the church at Culross. However, as William Skene explains in *Celtic Scotland*, the events of Serf's life place him nearly two centuries later and the church he founded was not the one that Mungo knew.

What has been forgotten is the pagan resurgence of the 540s AD which practically wiped out Christianity in northern Britain.

Chapter six

Mungo's childhood coincided with the later years of the unique period of tranquility in Britain known as "Arthur's peace." The long wars to drive back the three invasions by Picts, Irish and Saxons had ended at the great victory of Mount Badon when the British battle-leader Arthur shattered the Saxon army.

There are conflicting theories about "Arthur," but this is not the place to discuss them. Historically, the chief ruler in Britain at this time was a person named Arthur, whose title in Latin was "Dux Bellorum" ("Battle-leader"). In Welsh he was called "Guletic" ("Commander-in-Chief").

However, after 20 years that have lived in legend as a golden age, the popularity of Arthur's government was on the wane. A new generation had grown up who had no memory of the wars. New ideas sounded attractive and the beliefs of the Pagan Party made many feel they had more in common with the pagan Picts and Saxons than with their fellow Britons who were Christian. This was the rift that was forever the Britons' worst peril.

About 537 the conflict broke into full-scale rebellion. An alliance of rebel Britons and Picts took the field. They were led by a prince named Mordred. The only historical man of this name was the son of King Loth, who now ruled Dunpelder as his heir. He was therefore a brother or half-brother of Tannoc and uncle of Mungo.

For a full-scale revolution against Arthur's government, Mordred's first need was to amass a sizeable war-chest. This could only be collected in the more prosperous south of Britain. Perhaps Mordred and his Pict allies had been doing this and now hurried north to store the booty safely in the land of the Picts. Small hoards of treasure could be hidden in a secret cache to be recovered later. But most of the loot was ''on the hoof'' — slow-moving cattle and columns of slaves which must pass through the Antonine Wall by the Gate at Camlann to reach safety in Pictish territory.

News of these movements must have reached the Commander-in-Chief swiftly wherever he was on the long defensive perimeter around Britain. As Mordred's raiders hurried north along the bank of the Forth, these events would have touched the lives of Tannoc and Mungo closely. Without question the good priest of Culross hid Tannoc and her son in a place of safety. Indeed the whole Christian village was at risk while the pagan host passed by.

Mordred was in a frantic race to hurry his looted cattle and captives through the Camlann Gate before Arthur's cavalry could arrive from Carlisle. He lost the race. Arthur's horsemen had little more than 100 miles to ride, most of it along Roman roads. In a couple of days they had crossed the Antonine Wall and apparently attacked Mordred from the north, cutting off his retreat. In the desperate fighting Mordred met his end. But the great battle-leader Arthur also fell, mortally wounded. Camlann was a decisive victory, but without victors. Arthur's army held the battlefield, but the brain and hand that guided the struggle were gone.

Not long after the battle, in about the mid-500s, there arose on the battlefield of Camelon (the modern spelling) a Roman temple-like building which looked very like a victory trophy or a mausoleum for a hero. It was north of the Antonine Wall and faced south. It was remarkably similar in architecture to the mausoleum built by the Emperor Theodosius at Ravenna in 530. For centuries the domed tower stood near Camelon and was called by the local people ''Arthur's O'on'' (''Arthur's Oven'') because it looked similar to a clay bread oven. As young Mungo grew up in Culross he must have known it well as it stood in clear view only seven miles across the river.

The tower stood there for 1,200 years until in 1743 an iron merchant, wishing to build a factory at Camelon, knocked it down. It was the archaeological scandal of the age! Fortunately Scotland's leading archaeologist, Sir John Clark, had long been interested in the O'on and had measured and sketched it from every angle. In 1760 he built a full-scale replica at his estate of Penicuik House near Edinburgh, where it now stands.

Chapter seven

As Mungo grew to manhood, he learnt the skills of a river boatman, the arts of a fisherman and of a woodsman. But his chief study was the Gospels and the services of the Church. As soon as he was old enough he was ordained a deacon and assumed much more of the pastoral duties of the parish. There is no record of which bishop ordained him priest, but the probability is strong that it was Bishop Nevydd, a grandson of the saintly Brychan, King of Manau. Nevydd was "Bishop of the North" with his see at Falkirk, which was just across the river and only six miles west of Culross.

Like many a young priest, Mungo may have had day-dreams of being called to some glorious, sacrificial task. Instead he was called to visit an old priest who was not very well, and who lived seven miles upstream. Fergus, the priest at Carnock, was old and getting frail. Someone ought to visit him.

Telling his mother he would be home by nightfall, Mungo set off in his boat. He found Fergus feeding and watering his stock and was rather shocked by how much the old man had failed since last they met. He made up the fire and cooked supper and the two sat and yarned about Fergus' home on the River Clyde where the great missionary St. Ninian had founded a church nearly 100 years before.

Having someone to talk to cheered the old man up, so Mungo decided to stay the night. After midnight the old priest suffered a fatal seizure. As Mungo held him in his arms giving him the last rites, Fergus whispered, "Promise you'll bury me at the old church hallowed by St. Ninian beside the Clyde." Then he died.

It was a good day's walk to the Clyde, but how to take Fergus' body? There was a wagon in the yard and in the pasture two young oxen. Fergus had told Mungo he had never had the strength to train them to work in the yoke. First, Mungo laid the corpse in the wagon. Then he petted and talked to the oxen; he led them to the wagon where they seemed to understand what had happened to their master. Docilely they accepted the yoke and harness and by instinct followed the west road that led back to their old home on the Clyde. It was sundown when at last they halted at the little church beside the Molindinar Burn where it runs into the Clyde.

Neighbours gathered. Most were elderly and had known Fergus. There were practically no young folk. They looked sad and discouraged and said they had not seen a priest for several years. There was fear in their eyes.

Next morning they gathered again as Mungo buried Fergus against the church wall. He had intended to start for home right after the funeral, but in the meanwhile he had seen something that explained the fear in the people's eyes. In clear view four miles down the Clyde was a steep bluff and on its crest were large megalithic rocks. This was Craigmaddie Moor, the site of the most famous Druid altar in North Britain. Of late the activities of the Druid priests and soothsayers had greatly increased and people lived in dread of their satirical attacks and prophetic curses.

As Mungo looked at the sad faces of these Christians — a flock without a shepherd — he knew he could not go back home. Young Mungo was learning the lesson that God can lead a man who is willing to take on the job that needs to be done. So the young priest spoke to

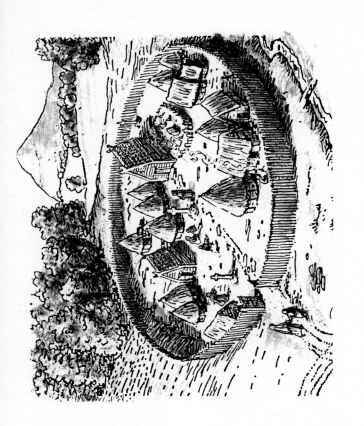

*An imaginary view of
St. Monenna's convent
near Traprain Law,
after a drawing by
Liam de Paor*

The ruins of the town wall of Dunpelder high on the side of Traprain Law

the elders and offered to stay if they wished it. They welcomed him gladly, though a few muttered that he had come too late. Mungo arranged to send a letter to the priest at Culross and to his mother.

Angwen, one of the few young men who came to church, offered Mungo the hospitality of his home and they became close friends. But his brother Telleyr was a sore trial. Loud-mouthed insult was his only conversation. He ran with a wild gang whose members repeated every slur and satirical comment they learnt at Craigmaddie Moor. Mungo tried everything to catch his interest and win his friendship. Sadly enough, in one of his gang's madcap escapades, Telleyr lost his life. Angwen suggested they give him Christian burial and they laid him close to Fergus where Mungo committed his soul to God. Some blamed them for this act but they replied, ''Forgive us our sins as we forgive those who have sinned against us.''

After a few weeks a new activity and bustle was noticeable in the homes around the church. Life was returning to the village. This small community had first come into existence because the Roman road crossed over the ford of the River Clyde and here a small fort called Cathures had been built to defend it and a cluster of houses had grown up around it. The Roman military had been removed long ago, so not much traffic moved along the road, and even the occasional peddler excited interest. One day a peddler leading two ponies arrived from the east, with a woman riding one of the ponies. She dismounted at Cathures and asked where she could find the priest Mungo. Thus word reached him that his mother had arrived.

Tannoc had come to make a home for Mungo and help in his work, and soon her warmth had drawn the farmers and fisher-folk, who were their neighbours, into a family circle. She was welcome in every cottage and hut, a favourite with the children and old folk alike. She was not sure she approved of her son's living quarters — a tiny hut against the west bank of the Molindinar stream, his bed a hollow in a rock and his pillow a stone.

His clothes were goatskin, the same as those of most working folk. Over them he wore a white alb and cowl with long tight sleeves, the dress of a priest, and he carried a shepherd's crook. He bathed in the stream every morning, as his mother had taught him. Every day he recited the whole Book of Psalms. In Mungo's day, learned men had wonderfully trained memories. In a world where there were few books, they carried a library in their heads.

It is likely that it was Tannoc who first called their church congregation "Eglais Cu." Literally in her Welsh tongue it meant "The Beloved Church" — not meaning the building, but the people as a family. The name has lasted a long time. Today it is pronounced "Glasgow."

Chapter eight

At Cambuslang, four miles up the Clyde from Cathures, lived a well-known priest and teacher named Cadoc. He came from South Wales but had worked a great deal in Ireland, where he had taught Finnian of Clonard, "the doctor of wisdom who trained the Twelve Disciples of Ireland." Mungo's life was deeply influenced by his friendship with Cadoc from this time on.

What was Cadoc doing on the Clyde? One of his students was a gifted scholar named Gildas, whose father King Caw ruled a minor kingdom on the Bannockburn. Theirs was a large family and Gildas wanted to recruit all his brothers and sisters to work for the Christian cause. With Cadoc's help he succeeded.

A tale Cadoc told about a mouse endeared him to Mungo. Once Cadoc was completely out of food. He was sitting very hungry in his cell praying, when a mouse came out of a crack in the wall and placed a little golden object on the floor in front of him. The mouse scurried away to the crack and brought back two, five, six more. There was a hoard of corn hidden in the crack. The mouse wanted to share it with him. Cadoc and the mouse became friends and thereafter shared their provisions.

* * *

Down river 15 miles, where the Clyde widens, rose the dominating twin crags of Alclyde or Dumbarton, the fort of the Britons. The king who ruled Strathclyde from this fortress was Rydderch Hael ("the Generous"). He was a Christian and men said he was a good one.

Mungo sailed down the river to pay his respects. The king and Mungo were exactly the same age and immediately felt a bond of comradeship. Rydderch of necessity had become an experienced and capable warrior. He had inherited his kingdom while still a boy and at once all his neighbours had tried to grab bits of his territory. It was a rough schooling. Rydderch's and Mungo's friendship, which began at that first meeting, grew steadily and in the end influenced the history of their country.

But all the neighbours were not so friendly. The patron of the Druid altar at Craigmaddie Moor was an ambitious and ruthless minor king, Morcant Bulc. He was a bitter enemy of Rydderch Hael. That autumn at harvest time Morcant sent out his war-band to raid the Christian farmers, looting all their crops and even driving off their draft animals. The looted grain was snuggly stored in Morcant's large royal barn.

That winter there was hunger among the members of the ''Eglais Cu.'' Mungo walked over to Craigmaddie Moor and faced Morcant Bulc, saying that the people needed food. Mockingly Morcant replied, ''You Christians teach that your God will provide for those who serve Him. I do not serve Him or believe in Him, yet I have plenty of food. You and your people are starving. Your teaching is false. Tell your God to transfer the food from my barn to your barn and if He does it, I'll be a disciple.''

Empty-handed Mungo returned to Cathures and gathered his people to pray. As most people know, it can really rain during a Scottish winter. That winter the skies opened and it poured and poured. The little streams roared with white water, the burns flooded their banks and Morcant's bulging barn took off towards the Clyde like an ark on a wild cruise. On the banks of the Molindinar it went hard aground beside the church.

Next morning Mungo gathered his ''Eglais Cu'' to thank God and eat a good breakfast. Morcant did not find it at all funny!

Chapter nine

A serious threat was developing. The ruler of Hadrian's Wall, one of the Coelian kings who reigned at Corstopitum (now Corbridge), was Gwendoleu, the recognized leader of the Pagan Party in the north. Across the wall from him lived the powerful Selgovae tribe, traditionally pagan and anti-Roman. Gwendoleu had wooed them and won them as allies, by paying special attention to the influential Druid wise men, who worked their spells high on their sacred mountain of Hart Fell. The most famous of these sages was Merlin.

In the annals of mythology there is no more potent figure than Merlin, the famed seer of Hart Fell, who was now Gwendoleu's bard, advisor and later his Arch Druid. There is a faint tradition that, at Mungo's suggestion, King Rydderch invited Merlin to visit him at Alclyde and Merlin came. Perhaps king and priest hoped to win the heart and mind of their most formidable and brilliant opponent.

In the 540s King Gwendoleu and his Selgovian allies were powerful enough to attack Reged, capture Carlisle and drive out the Christian King Cynfarch and with him the bishop and clergy of Carlisle. There had been a bishop at Carlisle for over 200 years.

The raging pagan storm sweeping across the north would not be halted. The saintly King Brychan had died and left his two sons, Rhun Dremrudd and Rhawin, as his heirs to rule Manau, the area around Stirling. War-bands of Picts and Saxon pirates ambushed and murdered them both. The violence swept on. A pagan mob seized the town of Falkirk. Bishop Nevydd, son of Rhun, boldly faced them in front of his church and died a martyr's death. The church was burnt over him.

These killings were a blow to the faithful at Cathures, Mungo feeling most keenly the death of Bishop Nevydd who had ordained him.

Sometime during this harrowing period Tannoc died. She could not have been over 40 years old. Perhaps she had suffered from some internal damage due to her terrible fall from Traprain Law.

Mungo was distraught. She had been his only parent, teacher, closest companion and friend. His abiding love for her shows in the number of places which bear her name in Glasgow and in Cumbria. She was buried by the Molindinar where St. Enoch's chapel was later raised to honour her. In Glasgow, Trongate and Tannochside as well as St. Enoch's Station salute her memory. (St. Enoch is a corruption of Sain(t T)annoc.)

King Rydderch summoned Mungo to Alclyde to confer urgently. News had reached him that a force of pagan Picts and Irish had captured Ninian's famous monastery at Whithorn. The abbot had managed to get the monks and nuns safely away by ship to Ireland but the price-less library had gone up in flames and smoke. The loss was irreplaceable.

Far worse, this meant that there was no longer any bishop in all the north and therefore no one to ordain new priests. Without priests the Church would wither away.

Rydderch had already acted and sent a letter to his mother in Ireland. She was a princess, influential in Church circles. He begged her to get a bishop to come across and consecrate a bishop for Strathclyde. Mungo approved but doubtless pointed out that Canon Law required three bishops to consecrate a new one. In critical situations in the mission field, this could be overlooked and Rydderch argued that this was just such a critical case. But Mungo was startled to find that the king proposed that he, Mungo, should be made bishop. A bishop was supposed to be at least 30 years old. Mungo was only 25. The king replied that without a bishop the Church in the north would die out. "There isn't anyone else."

The fact that Mungo was only 25 when made bishop firmly lodged in folk-memory. The murder of Bishop Nevydd and the driving out of the monks from Whithorn occurred about 550. This gives a check-point for dating.

An Irish bishop arrived by sea, nervous and eager to return home as soon as he could. There was no time for any pomp or ceremony, but rather an awe-inspiring sense of urgency and dedication. "Be to the flock of Christ a shepherd. Hold up the weak, bind up the broken, bring again the outcast, seek the lost." With all his soul Mungo answered, "I will, God aiding me."

Chapter ten

Not long after Mungo's consecration, a rowdy, insulting mob of horsemen clattered into Cathures, led by Morcant Bulc, who was grinning with triumph. Mungo went out to face him. Morcant could scarcely wait to break the news. "Your royal friend," he crowed, "is sailing into exile and I am now master of the great fortress of Alclyde. I am King of Strathclyde!"

Riding with Morcant was a young man named Caten. He was a grandson of King Loth and the present ruler of Dunpelder. He was Mungo's cousin but he had not come on a friendly family visit. He manoeuvred his skittish horse up to Mungo, kicked out with his stirruped foot and struck Mungo in the chest, knocking him down. "You bastard bishop!" he shouted as he rode away.

With that blunt and unmistakable warning, Morcant Bulc and his jeering mob rode off. Mungo got to his feet, wiping the mud from his habit, and walked slowly back to his church.

* * *

At this point in Mungo's story there is an hiatus. Few facts and traditions and no records bridge the next events. Jocelyn of Furness, writing about 1181, states: "Mungo was driven into exile by the malice of Morcant Bulc. Mungo therefore set out for Menevia in Wales to join St. David who was Bishop there. When Mungo reached Carlisle he heard that idolatry was rampant in the Cumbrian mountains and he turned aside, and, God helping him, converted many from strange beliefs."

Carlisle at that time was held by King Gwendoleu, the leader of the Pagan Party. It was a place that Mungo had to avoid at all costs. How gleeful the king would be if the Bishop of Strathclyde walked into his trap!

We can say with confidence that Mungo did not pass through Carlisle. How then did he get to Cumbria? The Roman road from Glasgow ran 80 miles south-east to Carlisle. But halfway, at a place now called Crawford, the main road was joined by a side-road coming in from the west. It was more a wagon trail than a road and it ran to the head of navigation on the River Nith. Here, small ships off-loaded cargo onto ox-wagons. So here Mungo might find passage in a ship that would carry him across the Solway Firth to the Roman port of Alavna (now Maryport) on the north coast of Cumbria. Carlisle would be avoided.

This is deduced from the map. However, it is interesting that, at the head of navigation on the Nith on the western side of the river, there is a place called Capenoch ("Enoch's chapel"). As we have noted before, in Scotland the name "Enoch" is almost always a form of "St. Tannoc."

Mungo was leaving Cathures, perhaps forever. Surely he prayed at his mother's grave. She must have been much in his mind. If some faithful friends gathered by the river to bid him farewell, might he not speak to them about his mother's indomitable faith? A chapel might later rise to memorialize the event. But to track the flight of a fugitive is never easy. This is no more than a "maybe."

Chapter eleven

Cumbria was unfamiliar country to Mungo and his friends, very different from the valleys of the Forth and the Clyde. Here mountains rose imperiously into the skies, their skirts draped with dense forest, the whole scene reflected in glittering lakes — breathtaking beauty, yet with a shiver of menace. As Mungo and his companions trudged through the dales they found the inhabitants of the occasional clusters of huts unfriendly and wary of strangers. Nor could they miss the many pagan symbols displayed.

Their route lay among awesome crags but it was the only way to bypass Carlisle and reach Voreda (Penrith). Here was the headquarters of Prince Urien, champion of the Christian cause and heir of the exiled King Cynfarch of Reged. From here Urien conducted his government-in-exile for the Roman Party. Therefore, if Mungo wanted to launch a mission in Cumbria, it was essential for him to have the prince's permission or, better still, his support.

It must have been an interesting meeting between these two men. Urien has been called the father of Prince Owen, Mungo's father. Was Urien therefore Mungo's grandfather? This is unlikely as there is a conflict of ages and Urien and Owen seem more like contemporaries than father and son. Genealogists of those times did not fabricate; they adapted the convention that made no clear distinction between a pedigree and a "King List." Each Roman Emperor was called the "son" of the former — the man from whom he inherited his power.

The Britons followed the Celtic custom of regarding the eldest son of a man's natural family as his heir. At this period the two customs, Roman and Celtic, were in the process of merging and it makes genealogical tables, like the Triads of the Welsh Saints, very confusing.

Urien came from a Roman British military family, one
of many claiming descent from Coelius. It is likely that,
following the Roman practice of adopting heirs for political
and other reasons, Owen was Urien's adopted heir, not
really his son.

At any rate, from this time on Urien seems to have
accepted Mungo as "family." The most important outcome of this Penrith visit was the confidence that grew
up between the two men. The prince was the most states-
manlike of the British leaders of that generation.

Urien explained to Mungo the strengths and dangers
of Cumbria, introduced him to trusty leaders and discussed
strategy. Perhaps Mungo had intended to pass quickly
through on his way to Wales, but when he heard of the
swift growth of pagan influence in Cumbria he realized
that the battle must be fought now — or never. So he
and his men turned back to the fells and dales of the Lake
District, spending the next three years there.

Where did the inhabitants of this wild woodland come
together to meet? At their village wells. Every man and
woman came at least once a day for water. And here they
also came for news, gossip and barter.

Mungo brought ear-compelling news and, as he journeyed from well to well, crowds gathered. Not all welcomed him. Some came to jeer and to throw rocks. At
their sacred altars high on Castle Rigg near Keswick, the
Druid soothsayers called down black curses on the Christians. But at the wells there was good news: bitter neighbours were reconciled, thieves returned their loot, feud-
ing foes made friends. And these miracles seemed to be
infectious. They passed over the hills and broke out afresh

in the valleys beyond. The water of the wells was put
to a new use when the bishop came and used it to mark
converts with the sign of the Cross.

In Cumbria it is easy to walk in Mungo's footsteps
because most of these ancient wells still exist and now
keep company with a chain of fine old stone churches,
built later to serve the congregations that for generations
had gathered at the wells. At Dearham near the coast
St. Mungo's church contains a very early font almost
resembling a village well that has been carried bodily into
the church. At Caldbeck a waterfall pours from a hillside
into a stone bowl in a charming garden setting. Mungrisdale bears the saint's name and his church there is small
and jewel-like.

But some of the wells are sad. One has been hidden
under concrete to prevent cattle falling in. Another has
been made almost unapproachable by the barbed wire
and nettles which surround it. Yet the romance of these
wells is very moving. Here, about 550, St. Mungo marked
with baptism our early ancestors. Here they first learned
to call God "Our Father," and first declared "I believe."
Surely these wells are national archaeological treasures
beyond price? One yearns for a little weeding and gardening around them, perhaps even a yearly pilgrimage of
thanksgiving when the wells can echo again to the music
of hymns and may again lend their water to baptize
a child.

The rapid spread of the Christian faith through Cumbria
alarmed the Druids and they appealed to Gwendoleu, the
pagan king of Carlisle. But he had no intention of getting
his soldiers entangled in the trackless gullies and swamps
of the Lake District. Better for him to attack Prince Urien

and drive him out of Penrith and conquer Lancashire as a kingdom for his warlike younger brother, Elifer.

Once again Mungo realized that the time had come for him to move on to Wales. But he was determined not to go until the Christians had lit a beacon that would burn on in the memory of the people of Cumbria.

So he summoned a great assembly of dedication for all the faithful. He chose the site with care — a clearing in the forest between Bassenthwaite Lake and Derwent Water. It was a high place with a good view. Here he raised a great wooden Cross, big enough to be seen from the top of Castle Rigg two miles to the east. There, surrounded by a circle of towering menhirs, stood the Druid's sacred altars.

On the day of the assembly the pagan soothsayers and priests looked to where the Cross stood. Down every valley and trail the people came by their hundreds — woodsmen, hunters and herdsmen, nobles and their servants, men, women and families. And as they came they sang and the lakes gave back the chant. No one had ever seen such a gathering and none who saw it ever forgot what happened at Crosthwaite in 553.

Chapter twelve

In Jocelyn's account of Mungo's journey from Cumbria to Wales, it says: "He directed his steps by the seashore and through all his journey scattered the seed of the Divine Word, gathering in plentiful harvest unto the Lord. After many days they reached Menevia and were welcomed with open arms by St. David." Some books take this to mean that Mungo followed the Cumbrian coast from Maryport to Barrow-in-Furness, but on that route there are no church dedications to Mungo. However, on the Lancashire coast at Blackpool, there is a dedication, and at Lancaster Cathedral, St. Mungo's Day is annually observed on January 13. The same is true of Liverpool Cathedral and there are other "footprints" that indicate that this is the seashore that he travelled. There does not seem to be any evidence to support the contention that Mungo went to Menevia or met St. David.

When Mungo reached Chester, he followed the River Dee up to Llangollen, then turned into the Valle Crucis and went north up the valley of the River Clwyd. He was then in the small kingdom of Tegeingl. It may be presumed that Prince Urien had urged Mungo to visit his father Cynfarch, the former king of Carlisle, who was living in exile there under the hospitable protection of his young cousin, King Cadwallon Liu of Tegeingl.

Mungo was welcomed here too as "family." Cadwallon was of Coelian descent and therefore was connected with half the minor kings in northern Britain, but he was a devout Christian. The senior priest of the mother-church of the Tegeingl tribe was the king's uncle, Asaph. He and Kentigern (in Wales, Mungo was always referred to by his baptismal name) at once became friends and comrades; for each of them the meeting was a moment of history. Old King Cynfarch may well have been alive to

MUNGO'S ROUTE TO WALES

c. 550-553

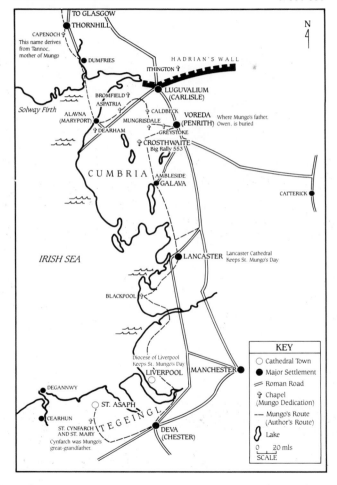

TO GLASGOW
THORNHILL
CAPENOCH ♱
This name derives
from Tannoc,
mother of Mungo
DUMFRIES
HADRIAN'S WALL
ITHINGTON ♱
LUGUVALIUM
(CARLISLE)
BROMFIELD ♱
ASPATRIA ♱
Solway Firth
ALAVNA
(MARYPORT)
♱ DEARHAM
CALDBECK ♱
MUNGRISDALE ♱
VOREDA
(PENRITH)
Where Mungo's father,
Owen, is buried
GREYSTOKE
♱ CROSTHWAITE
Big Rally 553
CUMBRIA
AMBLESIDE
GALAVA
CATTERICK
IRISH SEA
LANCASTER
Lancaster Cathedral
Keeps St. Mungo's Day
BLACKPOOL ♱
Diocese of Liverpool
Keeps St. Mungo's Day
LIVERPOOL
MANCHESTER
DEGANNWY
ST. ASAPH
CEARHUN
ST. CYNFARCH
AND ST. MARY
Cynfarch was Mungo's
great-grandfather.
TEGEINGL
DEVA
(CHESTER)

N

KEY

○ Cathedral Town
● Major Settlement
═ Roman Road
♱ Chapel
(Mungo Dedication)
-- Mungo's Route
(Author's Route)
◊ Lake

0   20 mls
SCALE

talk with Kentigern when he arrived, as the date of his death is not known. He is buried in the church at Ruthin which is named ''St. Cynfarch and St. Mary, Dyffryn, Clwyd.'' Saints in those days were not canonized officially by a Pope; they were so called by the unofficial public opinion of their neighbours. This king had kept the faith even though it cost him his kingdom and in the eyes of his neighbours he was a man worthy of the title ''Saint.''

Chapter thirteen

Kentigern's time in Wales is often spoken of as "exile," although he was with his own people all the time. But in a sense all Britons were exiles. Wars and plagues had harried them for two centuries. Some tribes had been driven from their home territory and had mingled with strangers. Others had fled in panic and lost all identity, dialects melting into a common patois as a new language took shape. The word "Briton" no longer indicated who they were. It was replaced by "Cymro" ("fellow-countryman"). The Saxons called them "Wal" or "Welsh," meaning "stranger." Kentigern/Mungo was a Cymro, a Welshman.

During this age of turmoil the Welsh produced a remarkable crop of Christian leaders. It is difficult to say where any movement starts, but the coming of Bishop Germanus gave it a mighty push. He was a Roman General and Governor of Amorica (Brittany). By popular vote the citizens of Auxerre chose him as their bishop and he obeyed. In 420 the Pope sent Bishop Germanus to Britain to counter the divisive Pelagian heresy. At St. Alban's he routed the heretical orators, then raised the morale of the army and, in 429, soundly defeated the army of Pict and Saxon raiders in the "Alleluia Battle."

During this time a Breton cavalry officer called Iltud came over to help the Christian cause. But what he saw of the behaviour of the "Christian soldiers" convinced him that Britain really needed not only better cavalry, but also better men. He left the army, became a monk and "turned Wales into a monastery," creating a new brand of Briton. His own monastery was Llaniltud (Llantwit-Major).

Britain urgently needed a new way of doing things. Along with much that was good the Romans had left behind a fatal political cancer. Rome had never discovered a peaceable method of passing on the royal power to a new government. Change of government was mostly accompanied by gross bribery, assassination and civil war. The Imperial Diadem passed to the new wearer besmirched with blood.

This model was being faithfully copied by all the petty military kingdoms in post-Roman Britain. To make bad worse, the Britons added a Celtic twist. By custom a king's children were farmed out to be brought up by foster parents. They grew up without personal knowledge of or affection for parents or brothers, without experience of a uniting family bond. When a king died his kingdom was divided between all his sons. Conflicts were inevitable between brothers who were strangers. The strongest son hacked his way to the largest slice of the kingdom over the corpses of his weaker brothers.

The young men who gathered around Iltud at Llaniltud to be trained were mostly from the ruling families of Wales. Iltud taught his pupils that only a profound moral change in men would cut to the root of the cancer. It had to start with themselves. Then they must dare to go out and tell the unwelcome truth to their own families and class.

One of Iltud's students was Gildas, Kentigern's friend, who had been driven out of home and country in the north by the pagan revolt. He retired to an island in the mouth of the River Severn to write *De Excidio Britanniae*. Few more damning indictments of a nation have ever been written. It was not just a crime sheet but also a bugle call to rouse Britons to build a better country. His charges were well founded. With blazing words he roasted the bishops: "Monsters of ambition, who buy for cash the office that should be earned by a holy life. You prance about haughtily preaching alms but never give a penny yourself. Judas in St. Peter's Chair!"

He named the "Five Evil Kings," of whom Maelgwn, the mighty king of Gwynedd, was the most powerful, and listed their crimes. He held little hope of real moral change in any of them, but for Maelgwn he had a wistfulness. This red-haired giant of a man had once been a monk at St. Iltud's school where Gildas had been his friend. But Maelgwn, seeing a chance to seize the throne of Gwynedd, had quickly cast off the monk's habit to don a royal robe. "The Enemy made you a Wolf like himself," wrote Gildas with tears of protest. "You reverted to your own vomit."

If Gildas was the Jeremiah of the Welsh revolution, St. David, Patron Saint of Wales, was the Joshua who raised and drilled an army of the new-type Briton. He looked for nothing good to come from any king. He wrote them all off and turned his hopes towards the common people. The one hope was to produce enough of "a new type of man," specially trained to do what others were unable or unwilling to do.

David moved his operational base from the comfortable south of Wales to the wild rocky shores of the southwest and founded his monastery there. His training of the spirit was based on hard physical labour, not imposed but accepted gladly to attain a purpose. David's men had to be as hard as nails and combat-ready.

The third of these revolutionary Welshmen was Cadoc. Perhaps he made the most difficult choice of the three. Himself the heir of a small kingdom, he did not think it enough just to damn evil kings. Someone had to govern and show how to do it properly. As Cadoc himself put it, ''If kings will not become saints, then some saints may have to become kings.''

When his father died and left him the kingdom, Cadoc did not feel he could walk away from his inherited duty. He was already abbot of his monastery of Llancarfan, so he became an abbot-king. He organized medical care for the sick, homes for the aged, widows and orphans, schools for the children and public work for the unemployed. Each day at his table he fed 100 poor, 100 widows, 100 clergy. He enlisted 100 soldiers and posted them in a fort overlooking the town. He trained them in new duties — to protect the defenceless, prevent kidnapping, looting and terrorism. For their day they were a new kind of soldier!

It may sound utopian but the people's needs were met not by bureaucrats, but by dedicated monks and nuns who served their neighbours ''for the love of God.'' The model of Llancarfan inspired many other cities and kingdoms in the centuries ahead.

When he was getting old, Cadoc stepped down as king, appointing as his successor a young man, Mouric, whom he had been training. He had no blood connection with Cadoc's family. He proved a splendid choice.

The actions of these men had inspired Kentigern and it was to communicate and cooperate with them that he had taken the road to Wales.

Chapter fourteen

Revolution in the soul moves quietly like yeast in dough but it moves with power. Iltud's most unsatisfactory student dropped out and went back home. He was Maelgwn, the red-headed monarch of Gwynedd. It is well worth following his story to watch how the yeast worked.

Soon after Maelgwn assumed his throne, a delegation of Picts came to him. In the Picts' system the royal power was handed on through the female line. The Princess Royal had the right to choose her consort and their son became the next High King of the Picts. The delegation requested Maelgwn to be the Princess's consort. Gwynedd would become the ally of the powerful Pictish nation.

Maelgwn accepted the honour and the royal lady duly arrived in Wales and stayed until a son was born. Although the king was hardly a model Christian he seems to have insisted that the child be baptized. Then wee Brude MacMaelchon and his mother returned to the land of the Picts and it is unlikely that his father ever saw his son or his consort again.

One classmate trained by St. Iltud, who kept in touch with Maelgwn, was his friend Deniol who visited him at his home. He found him apparently sitting on top of the world, powerful and rich. But as they talked Deniol sensed a wistfulness. Maelgwn admitted that he had taken the wrong turn in life and longed for another chance. So Deniol told him about his own dream, how he longed to build a monastery in the north that could do for young men there what Iltud had done for men in the south. Maelgwn came alive with enthusiasm and soon they were making plans. The king donated a splendid site beside the Menai Straits. The builders got busy and students flocked in. Maelgwn was in the middle of it. In 525 the monastery was consecrated and was called Bangor ("an enclosure like a sheep fold").

Unhappily King Maelgwn contracted a disastrous marriage. Relations were so poisoned that his rage went beyond control and he murdered his wife. Deniol found it necessary to get out of the kingdom quickly. He went no further than he needed to — just into the neighbouring land of Powis where he had friends and family. There he started all over again to build a new monastery, which was called Bangor-is-coed ("an enclosure in the woods"). Deniol's cousin Asaph was only 20 miles away in the Cantref of Tegeingl, so they always cooperated.

The ungovernable passions of Maelgwn broke out again and he murdered his nephew and then married the nephew's widow. He was an extraordinary mix — viciously homicidal and yet at the same time musical and artistic. At his banquets he always had 24 bards to entertain his guests. At his castle of Degannwy he staged the first bardic festival, the first Eisteddfod ever held.

Through his bardic interests the Pagan Party worked itself into his confidence. The pagan northern kings had been making rapid gains. Gwendoleu and his brother Elifer had driven Prince Urien out of Penrith and had conquered all Lancashire, of which Elifer now claimed to be king. It was a shock to all when Maelgwn gave his daughter in marriage to the upstart King Elifer.

Cadwallon Liu's minor kingdom of Tegeingl had an exposed coastline. When he learnt that Elifer was building a sizeable fleet, it naturally made him nervous. As a minor king, Cadwallon should have been able to turn for protection to his overlord who was Maelgwn. But Elifer was now Maelgwn's son-in-law!

Cadwallon, his uncle Asaph and Kentigern pondered these developments and prayed. ''Put not your trust in princes'' seemed sound advice. Instead they determined to establish in their own territory a monastery, ''a spiritual fortress,'' where brave men of faith could be trained as priests, preachers and missionaries and go out throughout the land to win pagans and lapsed Christians for Christ. Only such an audacious attack could match the peril.

They began at once to recruit the kind of men who could instruct in the training college and turned to men trained by Deniol, Cadoc, David and Gildas.

*Arthur's O'on (photo by Kenneth Lindsay,
by kind permission of Sir John Clark)*

*The Fergus Stone in the roof of the Under Church of
Glasgow Cathedral, showing the ox wagon carrying the
body of Fergus*

Alclyde, the capital of Strathclyde

Dolmen at Craigmaddie Moor, site of Druid worship

A spring flowing into a well outside St. Mungo's Church, Caldbeck, Cumbria

A ninth-century font in St. Mungo's Church, Dearham, Cumbria

An untended well near Hoddam, Cumbria

Crosthwaite Church, Keswick, where Mungo raised a Cross in 553

A circle of standing stones at Castle Rigg near Keswick

Chapter fifteen

Cadwallon promised to donate the finest locality in his lands for the new monastery and he took Asaph and Kentigern exploring through his forests to find it. Through the Cantref flowed the River Clywd, running north to the sea. Six miles from its mouth it was met by a tributary, the Elwy, flowing from the west. As the three friends entered the clearing where the rivers met, they saw a white boar rooting up the earth with its tusks, snout and hooves. It seemed as if this wild creature of nature was already digging the foundations for the monastery. Cadwallon donated the land to the Lord for ever and Kentigern probably put up a Cross. This was becoming his custom. They consecrated it to the glory of God and named the place Llanelwy.

The forest has eyes and news travels swiftly. Word soon reached the ears of King Maelgwn at his castle of Degannwy, 20 miles to the west. He was not pleased to have monks settling so close. His title as ruler of the Isle of Anglesey was ''The Island Dragon.'' It suited him well. One day, when Asaph and Kentigern were laying out the ground plan for the church, a very angry king and his cavalry escort came splashing across the Elwy.

"This is my land!" roared the Dragon. "You are trespassing by building on it. Pull down what you have begun, then begone and never come back!"

The land was owned by Cadwallon's Tegeingl tribe but the overlord claimed a right to it. Caution advised getting as far away from the choleric monarch as possible. But they had raised a Cross here to the glory of God. How could they pull it down just because a dragon roared? So they did not. They prayed and waited.

Some time passed and Maelgwn came back. This time the angry eyes were sightless. Maelgwn was blind. No tradition records what passed between the king and Kentigern. Did the bishop take the king's hand, stained by so much innocent blood? And did he help the blind man to reach out in contrition to grasp the hand of Christ, stained with "the Blood that cleanses from all sin"?

Tradition simply says that Kentigern prayed for Maelgwn and he recovered his sight. Another tradition states that Deniol also prayed for his blind friend. Doubtless Kentigern mobilized all the prayer-power he could. A message to Bangor-is-coed would have got all the monks on their knees.

Medical men recognize the king's condition as "hysterical blindness, brought on by violent emotional tension due, for example, to rage or guilt." It can cause a gush of blood or a stroke at the back of the head where the eyes are controlled, inducing blindness. If means are found to relieve the tension, sight may return. The pattern fits Maelgwn's temperament. The bishop helped him to face and confess his hate and guilt, and to accept God's forgiveness. The blind man was cured.

Compare the story of Saul of Tarsus on the road to Damascus. Both these blind men were cured. But more than that, the whole personality of each man was totally transformed. They accepted God's control. The ex-captain of a slave-ship, John Newton, wrote of this same miracle in 1780:

> Amazing Grace, how sweet the sound
> That saved a wretch like me!
> I once was lost, but now am found,
> Was blind, but now I see!

* * *

The next report we have of Maelgwn comes in a poem of the bard Taliesin, greatest of the early Welsh poets. He recounts that he sang at a banquet given by Maelgwn at his castle of Degannwy. Prince Rhun, his son and heir, hosted it with him. Among the guests were King Brochwel of Powis and his son Cynan. Son-in-law Elifer was not invited. The guest of honour was Prince Urien. At that time he was a king in exile, but he was also the battle commander of the Christian cause. The intention of the banquet was very clear — to send an unmistakable message to all Britain that the great King Maelgwn of Gwynedd had taken his stand firmly on the Christian side. It was the last act of statesmanship of this mighty Welsh king.

It is also from the bard Taliesin that we are given a last sad glimpse of ''The Island Dragon.'' In 540 AD yellow (bubonic) plague broke out in Egypt and spread rapidly. In two years it was killing thousands in

Constantinople, the world's largest city. This plague has been called the greatest of all the pandemics that undermined the ancient civilization. Cities and towns were abandoned in terror and never reoccupied. Agriculture stopped, the harvests rotted on the ground, law and social order broke down and fear alone reigned.

The bubonic infection was carried by fleas, borne on rodents that infested the grain ships. It spread inland from the ports and new outbreaks occurred about every half dozen years.

It appears that Maelgwn fell victim to the outbreak in 558. Taliesin recounts that, like many plague victims, Maelgwn "saw a phantom, a beast with yellow eyes, teeth and hair, and in terror he hid in the chapel behind locked doors and watched the monster through the keyhole." He then sank into a deep coma from which he never revived. Welsh folklore recalls "the long sleep of Maelgwn at Rhos."

Maelgwn's descendants ruled Gwynedd for a dozen generations after him. His son and heir Rhun succeeded to the throne and, from what is known of him, was a very capable leader. In 560 Elifer's fleet, backed by troops from other pagan kingdoms of the north, attacked Gwynedd. Elifer seems to have waited only until he knew Maelgwn was dead before attacking, hoping to drive Rhun out before he was firmly in control. But Rhun was ready, the combined attack was beaten back and Elifer was killed.

Rhun then led all the able free men of the tribal levies of Gwynedd, spearmen skilled in mountain warfare, on the four-month Long March, the story of which lives on in the legends of Wales. On their march northwards to the valley of the Forth they fought no battles and claimed no victories, looted and burnt no villages, took no slaves nor hostages. Rhun made his point convincingly — ''Better not meddle with the Welsh!'' — and he made it without spilling blood.

Any commander who could hold a levy of citizen soldiers together under discipline for so long was a truly great leader. But what caused him to behave like that? Had the change in his father so deeply affected him? Without question his actions were those of a Christian. Interestingly, at the old Roman fort of Caer Rhun on the River Conway, there is a very ancient church where services are still held on Sundays, and archaeologists suspect that it may be built over an even more ancient Celtic church.

Chapter sixteen

During this same period Kentigern and Asaph were creating the monastery at Llanelwy. Six hundred years later, Jocelyn of Furness wrote the story of its founding: "Kentigern had set his heart on building a monastery to which the scattered sons of God might come together like bees from East and West, from North and South." Young men, scattered throughout a hostile countryside, heard by bush-telegraph the news of the founding of the monastery. Many slipped quietly away from home to wend their way through the forests. Like the early Christians they were an underground movement. But they came by the hundreds, every sort of Briton, farm labourers and men of noble rank.

Jocelyn continued: "After prayer they manfully set to work. Some cleared and leveled land, others built foundations, carried timber, erected with skill a church of planed woodwork after the British fashion, enclosing it all in a *llan* or rampart and named it 'Llanelwy.' "

The number of monks who ultimately entered the monastery, says Jocelyn, was 965. These were formed into three groups: 300 of the unlettered men took on the farming and care of the cattle; 300 did the inside work — the cooking of the food, the carpentry and upkeep of the building and work in the workshops; 300 literate monks were charged with directing the divine services in church and teaching novices the all-important work of copying the Gospel. The influence of St. David's teaching and methods is clearly apparent.

The manual workers were in no way considered inferior. Manual work was worship. Agriculture, in which Kentigern was especially interested, was seen as playing a part in God's bounty. The cattle were treated with a kindness and care befitting fellow-creatures of the same Creator. Thus the monks became the innovators and improvers of agriculture, increasing the yield of food. This was vital in lands which were so ravaged by wars and plagues that most people lived on the edge of starvation. Most of the population were engaged in some form of agriculture, so the farming monks "preached by doing" to a wide audience.

Very soon the monks of Llanelwy received a major boost. Asaph's first cousin, Deniol, who was a bishop and a monk, returned to the monastery at Bangor Fawr on the Menai Straits, a dozen miles west of Degannwy. It became one of the major ecclesiastical institutions in Wales. Soon missionary monks were setting out from both these monasteries into the countryside to get practical experience for the stern tasks which lay ahead.

The Long March of King Rhun's army had reversed the momentum which since the death of Arthur had flowed towards the pagans, and it was again flowing towards the Christians. Another man whose influence was growing was Urien. He had a statesman's gift for weaving into alliance those who were at loggerheads. They said of him that he was the only man in Britain who could get his neighbours to unite to resist the Saxons. He made friends with Peredur, King of York, who commanded a powerful force of spearmen called "the Great Army," and who was the dominant power in central Britain. King Rhun married Peredur's sister and it may be that Urien played some part in this match.

When Elifer was killed at the battle of Caernarfon, he left behind a small son, Lywarch, whose mother was Rhun's sister. Urien might have seized the southern half of the kingdom of Reged which Elifer had captured from him, but instead Urien confirmed young Lywarch as king of this part of the country, thereby winning the young man's lifelong friendship and loyalty.

Rhun's behaviour on the Long March and Urien's treatment of Lywarch were giving Britain a new and nobler concept of what kingship could be.

Chapter seventeen

The same battle that the monks in Wales were fighting was also raging in Ireland. It was a war of faiths, Christ or Bel? Which would falter and fail? Which would survive and grow?

In Ireland the Druid forces rallied around the ancestral rites of the High King of Tara. In 544 a High King died and an election was held for a successor. The favoured candidate was Columcille, a prince of the royal line of the Ui Neill. Young, handsome and brilliant, a poet and sailor, he was eminently *rigdomna* (''king-worthy''). But he was a Christian and a monk. He was in training at Clonard, the school of the teacher Finnian, ''the tutor of the saints.'' The young prince was nominated for the sceptre of High King, but he declined the honour and chose to remain a simple monk.

The choice then passed to a prince, Diarmid MacCerbaill, but he was unable to muster enough support to put on the feast at Tara which was necessary to inaugurate a High King. He remained an unconfirmed king until suddenly in 558 he received all the support he needed, on one condition — that he accept the Arch Druid as his chief advisor.

The war of the faiths now intensified. It raged most fiercely around Columcille because, as a prince of the blood royal, he could always be chosen to replace the High King. So against him the Druids coined their most savage satires and bizarre libels.

By 561 the Pagan Party was seeking an open rupture with the Church in Ireland. Its chance came during the Teltown Games, held every fifth year. In addition to horse and chariot races and trials of strength and warrior skills, there was the fast, fierce game of hurley from which ice-hockey is descended. Playing in a hurley match, Curnan, son of the Christian King Aed of Connaught, accidentally struck and killed an opponent. In horror the boy fled and made his way to Columcille at his church of Kells. There he begged for sanctuary. By the Brehon Laws of Ireland the Church could grant sanctuary to a fugitive from vengeance until he could receive a lawful trial. But the Druids persuaded the High King to send soldiers after Curnan. They dragged the prince out of the church and murdered him.

Columcille slipped away, evading pursuit in the mist of the hilltops, and reached safety at Derry.

Curnan's murder meant war — just as the Druids had hoped. King Aed called out the men of Connaught, but all the Christian tribes of the north and west also mobilized. They realized that Diarmid and his Druids intended to break the power of the Christian clans for ever!

Diarmid marched his army right across Ireland as far as Sligo and the Atlantic coast, hoping to cut the Connaughtmen off from their northern allies. But he found the united Christian army drawn up in the narrow pass between the ocean and the mountain of Ben Bulben.

Among the gorse on the moor of Culdremne, the pagan army formed up while Druid priests drew around them an *airbhe*, a magical line that no foe could cross and live. Meanwhile, along the Christian ranks was carried a psalter written in Columcille's own hand, the symbol of the faith they fought for. This book, always called the *Cathach* (''Battle Book''), may still be seen at the Royal Irish Academy, Dublin.

The Christian warriors had been strictly commanded to maintain their ranks at all costs. They marched forward like one man, crossed the *airbhe* unscathed and marched on. Seeing this, the Druid ranks broke in rout. In their flight 3,000 men fell.

What is surprising in the record of this battle is that there is no word about vengeance. The Arch Druid and his priests were not hunted down. Even Diarmid was permitted to return to Tara and resume his reign.

But the magic had departed from the High Kingship. The Druids' power ebbed away. Diarmid abandoned the royal palace of Tara, remarking grimly, ''Woe to him who contends with the Church.''

Chapter eighteen

The men of Clonard and the other monasteries had stood together unbroken through the ordeal of the war and the common people of Ireland had rallied to them. The monks superseded the old Celtic heroes. The loud-boasting warrior of old, whose trophies were the heads of his neighbours, lost his popularity. The new Irish hero was "the saint," who lived to serve others and whose only trophies were the hearts of his neighbours.

But it was no time to relax. Across the Irish Channel, in northern Britain, the lights of faith had flickered out. Someone must dare to cross over and light them again. The Clonard men had studied the task but the first attempts to send out a mission were wiped out by pirates who infested the shipping lanes. Nonetheless, Columcille and his close friend Comgall, Abbot of Bangor in Ulster, continued to try. About 562 another attempt was made, this time led by Comgall's nephew Moluag. He was a Pict by blood and spoke the language. He located his mission in Pict territory on the long island of Lismore at the mouth of the Great Glen.

In all the north there had been only one pocket of Christians surviving: in the small kingdom of Dalriada, immigrant Scots from Ulster who had settled in the isles and lochs of Argyll three generations before. But in 558 the mighty High King of the pagan Picts had turned on the Scots, defeated and killed Gabhran, king of the Scots, and seized half their territory. This Pictish king was Brude MacMaelchon, son of "The Island Dragon" of Gwynedd. The babe baptized in Wales had grown up to be the most powerful king the Picts had ever had.

The new king of the Scots, who lived under Brude's unfriendly eye, was Conall, successor of the late King

Gabhran. He was a cousin of Columcille, and in his peril he sent him an appeal for help.

Columcille and his friends were praying to be shown the way to build a bridgehead by which the faith could return to Britain. Conall's message seemed like an answer to their prayers. The risks were great but nevertheless Columcille knew he must go.

He chose a dozen companions to make the journey with him. Most were kinsmen. They stowed the necessary baggage aboard a seaworthy, leather-sheathed curragh and sailed from Derry at the end of April 563, crossing to Kintyre and travelling up Loch Killisport to Delgon, the seat of King Conall, who welcomed them with rejoicing. They talked about the most strategic place to build "the bridgehead." It may have been Conall who suggested the Isle of Iona. He knew it well, as his father, grandfather and great-grandfather were buried there. The island, three and a half miles long by one mile wide, is just off the coast of the large island of Mull. It lay on the shipping trade routes, neither remote nor isolated, and above all it lay on the boundary line between the Picts and the Scots.

On the eve of Whitsun in 563 Columcille and his "Island Soldiers," as he called his companions, landed on the pebble beach at the south end of Iona. The campfire they lit that evening was the beginning of the rekindling of the Pentecostal flame in Britain. The islanders were already Christians, but the happy generous way in which the newcomers lived was something they had not seen before. Soon the whole region was talking about the happenings on Iona as the new monastery took shape.

Although Columcille spent his first two years travelling

through the mainland, helping the needy and defending the farmers against pirate gangs, he never lost sight of his primary purpose: to meet and win the formidable Pict High King. In 565 he felt the time had come for the attempt. He invited abbots Comgall of Bangor and Kenneth of Achabo to go with him, as both were Clonard men and both spoke Pictish.

There was no reason to expect a friendly reception, so they asked Moluag to take charge and carry on in case something went wrong and they never came back. The three abbots set sail on the 100-mile journey up the Great Glen to the High King's capital at Inverness.

When they reached the fortress gates, it seemed that their worst fears would be realized. The gates were closed and barred against them. Columcille walked up to them, made the sign of the Cross and knocked loudly. The written tradition states that by a miracle the bolts flew back, the gates opened and the abbots walked in.

Was there perhaps a guard on duty whose family the monks had befriended and who felt he could not deny entry to these holy men? At the risk of his life, did he pull back the bolts? What does it matter whether God touched the bolts or the heart of a guard? It was a miracle.

Shocked to hear that the priests were already inside his fortress, Brude made haste to welcome them and lead them to his hall. In the first conversation with the abbots, the king showed his full confidence in them by unbuckling and laying aside his sword. How to explain so swift a growth of trust?

Brude MacMaelchon must have known the story of his father's blindness and his miraculous cure, the transformation in his character and his championship of the Christian faith. He would also have known of his brother Rhun leading the amazing and bloodless Long March. He would have had full reports of the battle of Culdremne and its consequences in Ireland. He may have been eager to meet these remarkable Christians. He may have been prepared and waiting for them.

The abbots' mission to Inverness had a profound and lasting effect. Bede's *Ecclesiastical History of the English People*, the *Life of St. Comgall* and the *Pictish Chronicle* all state that Brude was baptized in the eighth year of his reign, 565 AD. Surprisingly, Adomnan's biography of Columcille does not say so. He does say, however, that Brude became Columcille's *amn chara* — a specifically Christian term meaning "soul friend." Possibly Adomnan knew of Brude's "infant baptism" in Wales.

At any rate, Domelch, Brude's daughter, was baptized at this time. She was the Princess Royal through whom the royal authority passed to the next heir. In consultation with her father she decided to exercise her prerogative to choose a consort. To the astonishment of all, she chose Prince Aidan, whose father had been King Gabhran of the Scots, killed in battle by the Picts. This act of Christian statesmanship laid to rest for ever the bitter hostility between the Picts and Scots, the unending blood feud.

Chapter nineteen

Like a thunder cloud the Picts had loomed over Britain for centuries. Then, like a flash of lightning, came the news of King Brude's conversion. How the news must have sped!

For the Scots of Dalriada it meant that their little kingdom would survive. For the monasteries of Iona and Lismore it meant that the gates were thrown open for the missionary monks. When Comgall returned home to Bangor in Ireland he surely sent the news to Deniol at Bangor in Wales, who passed it on to King Rhun, that Rhun's brother Brude MacMaelchon was now a Christian! What joy at Llanelwy when Kentigern, Asaph and Cadwallon heard it. Kenneth sent word to Cadoc and David, and they passed it on to Samson in Brittany. The like-minded men of this remarkable network gave thanks to God for this miraculous strategy in which they had all played a part.

In Strathclyde Kentigern's old friend Rydderch won back his throne of Alclyde after the death of the bullying Morcant Bulc. He no longer had to look anxiously over his shoulder for raiding Picts and he began to build a Christian alliance. The land of Manau on the upper Forth was subject to him, so he installed as sub-king his friend Aidan MacGabhran of the Scots, now consort to Brude's daughter, Domelch.

All across the north there was a turning away by the younger generation from the Druid philosophies of the Pagan Party; the pagan wave was ebbing and young men allied themselves to the Roman Party. Prince Nud of Dumfries sought alliance with Rydderch, as did Clytno of Edinburgh and even Mordaf, uncle of Caten, ruler of Dunpelder, who had once kicked Kentigern to the ground.

What was Kentigern doing in the midst of all these momentous events? Every year he, Asaph and Deniol trained and sent out into the field a steady stream of teachers and priests from Llanelwy and Bangor. A glance at the road map of North Wales illustrates their outreach. In Gwynedd alone there are over 100 places with names that begin with "Llan," denoting a Christian community — and these are just the ones that still appear on the road map. Most of the names derive from this period.

Each *llan* marked a group of literate and dedicated men or women serving God and their neighbours, praying, teaching the children, nursing the sick and comforting the dying, instructing the farmers in better methods for crop- and cattle-raising. It was a foundation for a new economy for Britain.

As already mentioned, a man who was influential in reconciling those at loggerheads and in drawing together the Christian alliance was Prince Urien, trusted by Peredur of York and by Rhun of Gwynedd. Through Kentigern's friendship Urien was also linked with Rydderch of Strathclyde.

In 573 tensions with Gwendoleu of Carlisle spilled over into open hostilities. Peredur led the Great Army north from York and with him went his ally, Dent of North Yorkshire. Urien with the Cumbrians and Welsh joined up with them. Rydderch and Aidan closed in from the north. The pagan army rallied at Carlisle and Merlin, the Arch Druid, used all his magic and oratory to stir up the pagan army to battle-pitch. His efforts earned him the high honour of a gold torque. About ten miles north of Carlisle beside the River Esk at Arthuret, the armies faced each other.

There Gwendoleu died and, although his men fought on fiercely even after he fell, the defeat was decisive and final. Merlin was so overwrought by the defeat that he lost his wits and wandered as a wild man in Ettrick Forest.

A tradition recounts that Kentigern travelled up into the Celidon Forest (Ettrick) to seek for Merlin and met him at Drumelzier on the headwaters of the Tweed. It seems in keeping with Mungo's character to go to the help of an old acquaintance in distress. But the suggestion that Mungo baptized Merlin seems as unlikely as Merlin's prophecy that Mungo would live to be 180 years old!

Another tale may have some truth in it. Merlin, no longer an awesome wizard but a sad and crazy old man, lived by stealing piglets from herdsmen and fish from fishermen's traps. The forest-folk were so angry with him that they chased him, throwing stones. He was cornered where the rivers Tweed and Ettrick join. He fell from the bank and was impaled on the spikes of the fish traps, and then drowned. Thus he died the three-fold death favoured by Celtic bards — a sad end for so brilliant a man.

Peredur of York withdrew his troops after the battle of Arthuret, leaving Rydderch and Urien to exploit the victory. For Urien it was a homecoming. He had been born in Carlisle and baptized with the name Urb-gen ("City-born").

Urien's reputation continued to increase. He stands out as the greatest and best-loved prince of his age. He was "the Golden King of Reged," chief of 13 other kings. He was "the pillar of Britain," the only statesman who could persuade his neighbours to unite and beat the Saxons soundly. His bard, Taliesin, who had come to him from Maelgwn's court, sang:

> Urien of Echwyd — most liberal of Christian men,
> Much you give to men of this world,
> As you gather so you dispose,
> Happy the Christian bards while you live,
> The stranger's refuge, battle champion,
> This the English know!

Chapter twenty

Back on his throne at Alclyde, the victorious Rydderch turned his mind to rebuilding a Christian nation. He no longer had to fear pagan attack from either north or south, though there were some hostile neighbours in the Edinburgh area. But there was nothing Christian to revive or build on. After 30 years of bullying rule by kings like Morcant Bulc, a whole generation had grown up with no notion of Christ's teachings. The very memory had been wiped out. As Jocelyn wrote, ''The Christian religion was completely destroyed in the kingdom.''

Rydderch turned to the one friend he felt could help and ''sent messengers to Kentigern'' to beg him to return to his former see. At Llanelwy, Kentigern laid the matter before Asaph, Cadwallon and the brothers. After prayer they all agreed that Kentigern must go — but not alone. This was just the sort of opportunity for which they had been praying and training. All who wished to volunteer should go with him. They knew that they would not be coming back. The road had no turning. The lands they were going to had recently been places of persecution and martyrdom — and could be again.

Of the roughly 900 monks at the abbey, 665 volunteered to go with Kentigern. Asaph was consecrated Abbot of Llanelwy. As senior priest of the tribe of Tegeingl, it was his duty to stay. He would continue the work of recruiting and training new monks. After a moving service of commissioning in the church, Kentigern led forth the gallant 600 by the north door, because they were going out to combat the northern foe. Thereafter the north door was opened only on St. Asaph's Day.

The monastic army started on its 300-mile march to the north, probably following the old Roman roads. They

Llanelwy — St Asaph

St. Asaph's, Llanelwy

must have received assistance and protection from kings Urien and Rydderch, and doubtless many Cumbrian converts came to meet Kentigern on the road. There are church dedications to "Kentigern" — the name by which the Welsh knew him — along this route which probably date from this time. Irthington at Hadrian's Wall, just north of Carlisle, is one of them. In West Cumbria, along the route he took southwards, the dedications are more often to "Mungo," the name he was called in Scotland.

Ten miles north of Carlisle the monks entered Rydderch's kingdom. The king had a royal castle at Hoddam on the River Annan and to this site he had summoned all the tribes of Strathclyde. It seemed as if everyone was at the rally — subordinate kings with their warbands, fishermen, shepherds, weavers, farmers, men, women and children. Above the timber palisade of Hoddam Castle streamed the Green Dragon banner of Strathclyde. Into the crowd marched the column of monks in brown habits, singing a joyful psalm. At their head walked the cross-bearer and behind him a strong stocky man of about 50 in the robes of a bishop. On a small rise stood the king and his courtiers. The old friends had not seen each other for 25 years. They embraced. Then before the eyes of his people the king took off his sword and belt, knelt before the bishop and put the sword into his hand, saying that he surrendered his realm into the keeping of Christ, the High King of Heaven. Never before in the British Isles had anything like this happened.

* * *

It may seem strange that Mungo did not immediately return to Glasgow but instead spent eight years based at Hoddam. But Mungo was a missionary bishop, not just responsible for one diocese alone. He reached out to Urien's people in Cumbria as well as to Rydderch's people in Strathclyde. Hoddam was located strategically for both. It became a place of continuous congress for the people of the north, for noblemen and plain folk alike. Teaching and training went on constantly and from Hoddam parties of Llanelwy monks went out along the coasts and up the valleys. Near Hoddam Castle in Annandale there are several ancient churches dedicated to Mungo.

As he had done at Crosthwaite, Mungo raised a large preaching Cross beside a well, the natural gathering-place. Folk began to call it "the Rood Well," now Ruthwell. Ships far down the Solway Firth could see it. It stood there as a rallying place for thousands of pilgrims. In 670 the wooden Cross was replaced by a stone Cross. Its carving is still one of Britain's most glorious works of art, and around the edges in Anglo-Saxon runic letters is written the poem *The Dream of the Rood*.

Chapter twenty-one

About 582 AD Mungo finally returned to Glasgow. Events in Britain suggest the reason for this. In 580 Adda, an English warrior, sallied forth with his troops from Bamburgh in Bernicia. King Peredur of York led out the Great Army to turn them back. They fought at Caergreu, a location now unknown. Peredur was killed, the Great Army totally destroyed. York, the strongest British city in the north, fell. The city which had sent Constantine the Great to rule the Roman world was no more. Its sudden collapse stunned the Britons and left a yawning gap in their defences.

King Urien swiftly rushed troops to Catterick, the vital crossroads commanding the routes to Carlisle and Scotland. Adda's victory encouraged the Saxon pirates in the Orkney Isles. For three centuries they had operated a profitable business of raiding the British east coast in alliance with the Maeatae Picts, the tribes of the coastal lowlands from Aberdeenshire to Fife. The firm hand of their High King, Brude MacMaelchon, had held them in check for a generation. But Brude was getting old and the pirates thought they might dare to sail again.

A rebel army of Pict and Saxon allies was at Circenn near Aberdeen in 584 when confronted by Brude with the royal army. Things did not go well and Brude was killed in the battle. He had been a trusted friend and had provided unfailing support to the Christian cause for over 20 years, and Mungo and Columcille mourned his passing. The pirates' victory exposed the Forth valley and Strathclyde to attack.

This may have been why Mungo moved to be closer to King Rydderch at Glasgow. Mungo came home to his little church on the Molindinar Burn, his ''Eglais Cu'' and his mother's grave. King Rydderch moved the royal dwelling down from the rock of Alclyde and built a new home at Partick, two miles north of Mungo, so that they could be in constant, close consultation.

It was over 30 years since king and bishop had worked closely together, and it was a strength and a joy to these old friends. Rydderch's wife had died some years before and he had just married a much younger woman named Laguoreth.

Around any royal court there are always noble young men eager to make themselves helpful and pleasant to royalty, hoping to be rewarded for their efforts. In the Celtic world, royal gratitude was often shown by the giving of gold rings. The queen however had no rings of her own, only those she had received from the king. On one occasion the queen, wishing to show gratitude, innocently but unwisely gave to a courtier a ring she had received from the king.

Soon afterwards the court went on a fishing trip along the banks of the Clyde. At noon they halted at a shady place for a meal and a midday nap. Here the king noticed on the finger of the courtier the ring he had given to the queen. Jealousy boiled in him. He waited until the courtier was fast asleep, then slipped the ring off his finger and angrily hurled it into the river. When they returned to the palace the king confronted the queen, demanding to see the ring. When she could not produce it the king ordered her locked in prison.

The poor woman in her despair turned for help to Bishop Mungo, pouring out her confession of guilt or foolishness. Mungo was wise and compassionate with people

Valle Crucis, North Wales

The Cathedral of St. Asaph, Llanelwy, North Wales

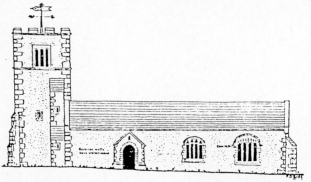

The church of St. Cynfarch and St. Mary, Dyffryn, Clwyd

Degannwy, King Maelgwn's stronghold

Valle Crucis, North Wales

The Cathedral of St. Asaph, Llanelwy, North Wales

The church of St. Cynfarch and St. Mary, Dyffryn, Clwyd

Degannwy, King Maelgwn's stronghold

The church built within a Roman camp at Caer Rhun

The battlefield of Culdremne

The shrine of the Cathach

St. Gregory's statue and table in St. Andrew's, Rome

*A statue of the Angel of Death sheathing his sword,
Hadrian's Tomb, Rome*

St. Martin's Cross at the foot of Tor Abb on Iona

and very wise in the ways of birds, animals and fish. Fish will strike at any shiny object and they constantly patrol the same stretch of water. Mungo enquired where the lunch halt had been beside the Clyde. Then he sent one of his monks, skillful with rod and line, to cast in the same place. He hooked and landed a large salmon. When the fish was cut open, there was the queen's ring!

Certainly it was a miracle — the miracle of a caring heart and an intelligent brain, both gifts of God. As a little boy Mungo had cared enough to help a fallen robin in its distress. As an old man he cared enough to help a fallen queen in her distress. It was all one, the motive and pattern of his life.

This story is recalled in the coat of arms of Glasgow and in carvings in St. Asaph's Cathedral, Wales. Since Mungo left no written words of his own, this story tells us much that helps us know him better. He justified his nickname: he was ''the beloved.'' He cared enough to save a queen's marriage. His caring saved a kingdom and a dynasty. But on that day Mungo was not thinking of the history books, but of one tear-stained girl.

* * *

A century ago an eminent historian, commenting on the story of Mungo and the salmon, declared: ''The story of the fish and ring is one of those hack incidents that come into many folk-tales about saints. There is, of course, no truth whatever in it.''

Nevertheless, from Canada comes this interesting corroborative story. On August 27, 1971, the *Ottawa Journal* printed a story about a 12-year-old boy called David. He loved to fish and had spent all his pocket money to buy a shiny new West River lure ($1.95 plus tax). He went up into the Gatineau Hills to Big Bear Lake to fish with his grandfather. He cast his line. Immediately a large pike struck at his lure. David tried to reel in but the pike dived, snapping the line, and he watched his lure disappear, twinkling in the dark green water. It was bad enough to lose his prize lure but, to make it worse, nobody would believe his story of the large pike.

A week later one of his grandfather's business partners went up to Big Bear to fish. He had heard the story of David's ill fortune so decided to fish in the same bay. At his first cast a large pike took his bait. The man was an experienced angler but it required all his skill to bring the fish in. It was a 6 lb. pike — and from its jaw dangled a shiny West River lure ($1.95 plus tax)!

David claimed no miracle but was very glad to have his lure back. No one can know, but perhaps an event similar to the one that occurred on a Canadian lake in 1971 also happened on the River Clyde in the 580s.

Chapter twenty-two

In his sixties, Rydderch was getting too old to command his army in the field. So he turned to his younger friend, the Scot Aidan MacGabhran, and invited him to lead the Christian forces of the north. Aidan was now King of the Scots, having been consecrated by Columcille at Iona in 574.

Rydderch and Aidan were both expecting trouble from the Maeatae Picts and the piratical Saxons from the Orkneys. After their victory at Circenn, where they had killed Brude, the pirates felt that the ''good old days'' were back again. Trouble came in 585 when the Pict and Saxon allies marched in full force towards Stirling. Aidan moved the Scots and the allied army to block them and, on the heights of Dumyat (Dun of the Maeatae) near Bridge of Allan, they fought in a slugging battle with no quarter given.

Back on the Isle of Iona Columcille called all his monks to prayer when he felt in his spirit that the battle was joined. In the evening, after a long and anxious day, the abbot rose to tell his men, ''Now there is victory — but not a happy one.'' Later, word came that, of the Scots army of 2,000 men, 303 lay dead at Dumyat. Among them was Aidan's eldest son, Arthur. But the back of the pirate alliance had been broken. Brude had been avenged by the Scots, once his enemies whom he had made his friends.

A respite of a few years was won by Aidan's victory at Dumyat. Then came the time for a sustained strategy by all the Christian forces to win the Lowland Picts. On Iona Columcille and his monks at once began to prepare. So did Mungo in Glasgow with his Welsh and Britons. Then word came that the abbot of Iona and his Gaels were coming to consult with the bishop at Molindinar.

Writing centuries later, Jocelyn of Furness shows how stirred he was by the word-of-mouth traditions about this meeting: "Saint Columba, a man wonderful for doctrine and virtues, earnestly desired, not once and away, but continually to rejoice in the light of St. Kentigern. He desired to visit him, come into close intimacy and to consult about the things that lay near to his own heart."

There is no record of the route by which Columcille came, but his preference was always to go by sea. He was never happier than when he was aboard ship with a brisk gale on his quarter. He brought with him a hand-picked force of Iona men including his very capable personal secretary Lugbe mocu Blai.

A small fleet of curraghs was sighted coming up the Clyde. Mungo rallied his "Eglais Cu" and went out to give the visitors a memorable welcome. He had never, so far as is known, met Columcille before. The Britons went forth with youngsters in the front, then adults and lastly the elders, all singing "How great is the glory of the Lord. The way of the just is made straight." The Gaels coming up from the boats replied in song, Columcille's glorious singing voice leading them, "The saints shall go from strength to strength. Alleluia!"

The two groups met at Mungo's Well, long to be seen off Gallowgate in Glasgow. There followed a festive meal. Mungo rarely ate anything but bread, cheese and milk and, if this is what he offered to Columcille, the abbot would have been quite content. Later there was a symbolic exchange between bishop and abbot, each giving the other his own pastoral staff as a pledge of unity.

Jocelyn catches the drama and excitement of this meeting, but he seems to have had little inkling about ''the things that lay near their hearts'' or the strategic purpose which had brought them together for consultation.

Chapter twenty-three

The central purpose of the consultation was this. How could they enlist the whole manpower and conviction of the Christian communities in the north to win their neighbours, the Lowland Picts? Rydderch would have been central in the discussions as would Aidan, whether he was at Glasgow or not. During the discussions Columcille's secretary Lugbe mocu Blai may well have impressed Rydderch, as a friendship began between them which was to be important later on.

One decision taken at this conference was to make Dunkeld the headquarters for their first missionary effort. It was the most easterly of Iona's missions, the closest to the Picts, lying on the flank of the great valley of Strathmore, the heartland of the Maeatae or Lowland Picts. The tradition of Dunkeld Abbey relates that for six months Mungo and Columcille worked together from Dunkeld. Their presence there endowed Dunkeld with such prestige that for centuries afterwards it was the premier church of the land that was becoming Scotland.

Studying church dedications believed to date from this period gives some indication of the lines of advance and shows the interlocking efforts of missions from all parts of the north. No such combined operation had ever been seen before, nor had such a corps of trained Christian teachers moved through the country.

In the Cairngorm mountains, five miles from Balmoral, is the church of Glengairn (Glen Kentigern) dedicated to St. Kentigern/Mungo. Twenty miles east of it is Lumphanan, a name derived from Llanfinan. Finan was one of Mungo's Welsh priests from Llanelwy. Seven miles east of that is Midmar, a dedication to Nidar. He was a Cumbrian cousin of Mungo's and a grandson of King

St. Kentigern Church, Glengairn, five miles northeast of
Balmoral, Scotland (photo by Nicholas Hall)

Urien. All these mission churches point east down the
River Dee towards Aberdeen.

Moluag of Lismore and his monks from Rosemarkie
and Mortlach extended their visitations along both coasts
of the Moray Firth and down Strathspey. With them
worked Drostan, Columcille's nephew, and Donnen, who
later died a martyr's death on the Isle of Eigg.

WINNING THE PICTS

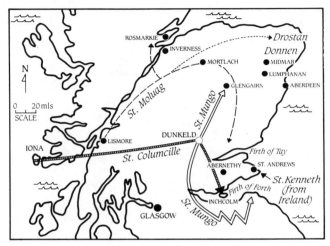

Between 585 and 590 the saints of the north from their base at Dunkeld launched a combined missionary effort to win the Lowland Picts. Columcille brought over the brothers from Iona to join with Moluag's men from Lismore and Mortlach. Mungo brought his Welsh from Llanelwy and Kenneth came with his Irish monks to found the monastery of Kilrymont, later called St. Andrews.

In the year 585 a new High King of the Picts was acclaimed. He was Gartnait MacDomelch, son of Brude's daughter. Though his father Aidan was a renowned warrior, Gartnait chose to bear his mother's name. Possibly he meant in this way to stress that he was first and foremost a Pict. For his capital he chose Abernethy on the River Tay, a place already sacred to the Picts. Gartnait brought priests from Iona with him.

Now Columcille moved his base from Dunkeld to the

Tay valley. About this time, the chief bard of Ireland, blind Dallan Forgaill, composed a majestic eulogy about Columcille's work. It was the first poem *written* in Gaelic: "Columcille taught the tribes around Tay, a river in Alban, and subdued to benedictions the mouths of the fierce ones who dwelt with Tay's High King." Gartnait was only about 20 years old when he became High King and he probably needed strong support to keep "the fierce ones" in line.

Other reinforcements came too. In the valley of the Tay is a dedication to Moluag, showing that he came down from Strathspey. Caten and his nephew Blane came over from the Isle of Bute. And from Ireland came Kenneth of Achabo, one of the three abbots who had gone up to Inverness to challenge and win Brude, Gartnait's grand-father. Kenneth, who spoke Pictish, led the work in Fife, the land south of Abernethy. He finally built his chief monastery on the craggy cliffs overlooking the North Sea. He named it Kilrymont ("church of the royal mount"), now called St. Andrews.

Then Columcille took the next step forward and moved his base to the Firth of Forth, placing his headquarters on the island of Inchcolm close to Dunfermline. The Abbey of Inchcolm remained a daughter-church of Dunkeld for centuries.

From here Columcille could again operate by sea, keeping in touch with Kenneth in Fife and with Mungo who was working in his homeland, the Lothians. There are numerous dedications to Mungo in East Lothian and around Edinburgh. But he seems to have met hostility from the royal family of Edinburgh — a "prophet being without honour" in his own home area.

* * *

As the years went by, it became certain that the Lowland Picts had been drawn into the new unity that was
embracing the peoples of the British Isles. The Cross had
been planted on the shore of the North Sea, so long the
highway of heathen pirates. From Cornwall and Wales
to the northern capes the Celtic peoples of the British Isles,
Briton and Pict, had returned to the Christian faith or been
won to it for the first time. The Celts had made their
decision and it would never be reversed.

Chapter twenty-four

Ahead loomed the next task, formidable but inescapable. How to win the English? Mungo, Columcille and their followers must have wrestled with that question. The barriers of racial hatred between Celt and Saxon were so high. The Britons wanted nothing to do with the English, whom Gildas called ''a race hated by God and man.'' Yet they must be won or Britain was doomed to an endless war of annihilation. However, a direct approach seemed out of the question.

Faith to move mountains — then the gleam of a thought. What if Rome could gain entry to the English from the south? Someone who could speak for the Britons would have to go to Rome to convince the Pope of this daring strategy. The roads to Rome had been barred for over a century by heathen war-bands wandering across Europe. But of late the nation of the Franks had accepted the Catholic faith and the roads and seaways, though hazardous, were again passable.

Bishop Mungo was now a man between 60 and 70 years old, yet he volunteered to make the attempt.

* * *

The matter of Mungo's journey to Rome has been much argued. In the early centuries it seems always to have been accepted as a fact, but during the Reformation there were many reasons for denying that Mungo ever went to Rome or met the Pope. Yet times change and what is unbelievable in one generation is acceptable in another. Who in Glasgow in 1882 would have believed that a Pope would ever visit Glasgow? Yet in 1982 Pope John Paul was warmly welcomed by the city.

Mungo's journey was regarded as a pilgrimage and its deeper purpose naturally kept confidential. Whether his party travelled by land or sea is unknown. It is about 1,300 miles from Glasgow to Rome — for a crow! This would take over six months for men to travel on foot, not allowing for delays by weather, war and weariness.

The Rome to which Mungo appealed for help was not the rich, powerful, authoritative papacy of later ages. Rome was a ruined echo of its imperial past. The Emperor and his court had long since moved to Constantinople. The once populous city had dwindled to a shabby town of a few thousand, huddled beside the muddy, malarial Tiber. The glory had departed; only the papacy was left.

Half of the Church in Europe held to the Arian heresy and was at enmity with Rome. France, nominally Catholic, was in a sad state. As St. Gregory of Tours charged, ''Many Gallic bishops are habitually drunk, embroiled in politics and obtained their Holy Orders by bribery.''

The Pope, Pelagius II, was a fine and able man but few who have sat in St. Peter's Chair have faced such a multitude of problems. He depended greatly on Rome's young governor, the Prefect Gregory. Daily they wrestled with the hunger of fugitives, robbery on the roads, mutinous unpaid soldiers, dishonest traders and polluted water supplies.

In the search for answers, Gregory's attention was attracted by the new concept of monastic life that St. Benedict was developing at Monte Cassino: ''God-centred men committed to serve others.'' Here, he felt, was the only hope of answering the poverty and brutal godlessness of Europe's society.

So he resigned as Prefect, turned his mansion on the Caelian Hill into a monastery, gave his wealth to the poor and became a monk. When barbaric Lombards destroyed Monte Cassino, Gregory welcomed Benedict's monks into his home.

But the Pope urgently needed his most able man to represent the papacy at the Emperor's court in Constantinople; therefore, in 578 Gregory was sent as ambassador. He was there for seven years. When he returned to Rome in 585 he brought some relics of St. Andrew the Apostle to enshrine in his monastery, which he renamed "St. Andrew's."

It must have been between 585 and 590, while Gregory was abbot of St. Andrew's, that an incident related by Bede occurred in Rome's slave market. English boys for sale as slaves stirred Gregory's first interest in the English race. "Not Angles but angels," he punned.

This was the Rome into which Mungo and his party tramped sometime in 590. They were dusty, travel-toughened and eager to lay their English-winning strategy before His Holiness. Pope Pelagius was ailing but he recalled that Abbot Gregory had spoken with interest about the English. So he sent Mungo's delegation on to St. Andrew's. "Gregory will be my successor anyway," he thought.

In the dining room of St. Andrew's stands a carved marble table at which Gregory used to teach his monks and wait on his dinner guests — usually the poor, homeless or unwanted. What discussions may Gregory and Mungo have had at that table, perhaps infecting Prior Augustine and the young monk Paulinus with their missionary enthusiasm? As a result, Gregory seems to have determined to lead a hand-picked group of missionaries back to Britain with Mungo.

There are records in Rome which show that Gregory did set out on the journey to Britain and went three days' march to the north. He had the Pope's permission to go. No man as experienced and responsible as Gregory would set off for unknown lands without trustworthy guides and interpreters. This raises the question: who were these guides and interpreters if they were not Mungo and his party?

On the third evening of the journey Gregory was resting under some trees when a locust jumped and landed on the breviary he was reading. The abbot's wit always turned to puns and plays on words. A locust in Latin is "locusta." The two words "locu sta" mean "stay in place." Gregory wondered if God was trying to tell him something.

Soon after, two tired horsemen on sweating horses galloped up. They had come at top speed from the Pope. Yellow plague had broken out again in Rome. Pelagius himself was smitten and dying. He had named Gregory as Pope-elect. With all his soul Gregory yearned to continue his journey, but he knew it was his duty to go back.

It would be hard to measure the grief and disappointment of Mungo and his companions. They had come so far in a year of travel and, just as success seemed assured, the effort had failed. And Gregory, whose whole soul was set on this great adventure, had to turn back to a plague-ridden city and the unending burden of public affairs!

But before Bishop Mungo and his British companions departed on their long homeward journey, Gregory gave Mungo a bronze sacring-bell, about four-and-a-half inches high, to be used in church worship. Perhaps it was his own. It survived in Glasgow until as late as 1661 and appears in Glasgow's civic arms. In papal letters of the twelfth century Glasgow is termed ''a special daughter of the Holy See.''

* * *

Before following Mungo and his fellow-travellers home to Britain, let us take a brief look at how Gregory fared back in the Eternal City.

Around the walls of Rome packs of thieving Lombards prowled, seeking an entry to break in and steal. From the gates flowed a stream of refugees escaping the horrors of the plague. Inside the city Gregory found a dead spirit of despair. Fear was the first enemy to be defeated.

The plague's first symptom was sneezing and a sneeze could set off a panic. Gregory proclaimed that, when people heard someone sneeze, they must say ''God bless you'' — thus focusing people's attention on God's help and mercy. Folk still say it today!

Frightened people tend to huddle in dark corners. But so do rats. Gregory had no medical knowledge that the yellow plague was spread by fleas carried on rats, but he did know that fear grows in the dark. So he organized seven huge processions, each to form up at one of Rome's major churches. They would process through all the streets for three days, finally assembling at Santa Maria Maggiore for a High Mass of forgiveness and dedication. All the priests, monks and nuns were deployed to marshal the processions, provide candles and lead the singing. As the torches lit the dim alleys the people of Rome flowed out of dark corners into the light; the singing gave them a feeling of festivity that banished the chill of fear. They were up and doing *something* and doing it *together*. During the first day's march 80 people fell dead of plague — but the march went on. The city was full of light and music. ''God bless you! God bless you!'' they sang.

On the third day, as the crowds crossed the River Tiber towards Hadrian's Tomb, people declared that they saw a huge Angel of Death sheathing his sword. That day the grip of the plague broke. The yellow plague had killed a third of Rome's population but it had not destroyed their courage.

Chapter twenty-five

At least two years passed before Mungo and his companions saw Britain again. Much had changed. His old friends Cadoc, Asaph and Deniol were dead. But it was in the north that the changes were most startling.

Mungo remembered that the English stronghold of Bamburgh on the North Sea had been a growing threat. King Urien of Reged, Mungo's kinsman and now Britain's most respected statesman, had moved to counter the danger. Using his diplomatic skill he wove together an alliance of Britons both of the Roman Party and of the Pagan Party. The hard core were the Cumbrians, Rydderch's Strathclyde troops and Aidan's Scots. Aidan recruited Fiachna of Ulster. But joining the army were also traditional foes like Guallauc from the Upper Forth and Morcant of Edinburgh.

It was Fiachna's Irish who stormed and captured Bamburgh. The surviving English fled to the isle of Lindisfarne. Urien besieged them there for three days until their food supplies ran out. Starving, their surrender was expected hourly. If the Britons stayed united the victory would be greater than Arthur's at Mount Badon.

But Morcant, grandson of Morcant Bulc who had driven Mungo into exile, seethed with jealousy against Urien. The victor of this battle would earn immortal fame. Morcant wanted that for himself. He paid a traitor called Lovan to stab Urien to death so that Morcant could receive the surrender of the defeated English.

The news of Urien's murder so shocked the Britons that they were unable to act. It cheered the English who seized their weapons again and fought on. The Britons' alliance fell to pieces as every kinglet and tribe hurried home to protect their corner or seek vengeance. Never again would the Britons achieve unity.

For a short while Owen ap Urien, Mungo's father, defended Reged from all attacks. But when he fell, Reged died with him. He is buried in Penrith. In grief Taliesin sang of him:

> Splendid he was in many-coloured armour.
> Horses he gave to all who asked.
> Freely he shared for his soul's sake.
> Lord, look upon his need.

* * *

In his life of Columcille, Adomnan tells a story about this period. Rydderch of Alclyde found himself surrounded by treacherous neighbours like Morcant. He feared for his own life, knowing that after Urien he was the next most likely victim of the pagans' treachery. He confided this fear to Lugbe mocu Blai, begging him to ask Columcille whether enemies would succeed in murdering him. Lugbe replied, ''Why ask what no man can know?'' But the king urgently persisted and finally Lugbe sent the message to Columcille on Iona. He replied at once to his old friend, ''Have no fear, for none of your enemies shall hurt you. You will die in your own bed with your head on a feather pillow.'' And that is how the gallant old warrior died 13 years later.

This incident must have occurred in 590 or 591. Rydderch's palace at Partick was only two miles from Mungo's abbey church. Why did the king not confide in his dear friend Bishop Mungo but instead speak of his

Tomb of Owen ap Urien, Penrith

trouble to a foreign Gaelic cleric? It would seem to imply that Mungo was not in Glasgow at the time but was in Rome. Knowing this, Columcille had sent his most trusty lieutenant to support King Rydderch during his bishop's absence.

From this time on the petty-kings of the Britons made mistake after mistake. The English never forgot the scare of their near-annihilation at Lindisfarne. They put aside their quarrels and united behind their best commander. They were soon able to recapture much of what they had lost, including the strategically important Catterick.

Chapter twenty-six

In his biography of Columcille, Adomnan tells of an event which must have happened soon after Mungo returned to Glasgow. He records that a papal delegation of seven priests arrived at Iona, sent from Rome by Gregory to visit Columcille. These must have been men who had intended to go to Britain with Gregory. When he had had to return to Rome to become Pope, he had asked them to visit Columcille at Iona.

It is a delightful story. When the Roman visitors arrived at Iona, the abbey was out of food. How mortifying for the generous-hearted abbot, who wished above all things to welcome and honour these special guests! Adomnan merely states: "Columcille prayed and food was miraculously provided."

A modern journalist longs to ask "What and how?" The answer is indicated by the stories we know of the way Columcille lived and acted.

There was Findchan, the bad-tempered neighbour who was angry with the Iona brethren. To placate him Columcille sent three measures of seed barley with the message "Sow it and trust God." That made Findchan madder still. "How can a crop succeed when it is past midsummer?" he stormed. But his wife said soothingly, "Why don't you do what the good abbot says?" Grumpily the farmer sowed — and reaped a bumper crop early in August. Findchan learned to trust God and thereafter in gratitude sent any surplus grain to help the brothers on Iona.

Colman was a poor Pict farmer with only five cows. Columcille discovered that pirates had repeatedly looted him. Columcille blessed him and his herd. Next time the robbers came they were caught in a squall and went down with their ship. Colman too sent his surplus to Iona.

Perhaps on the day that the Roman priests arrived at Iona, Findchan rowed over with his surplus barley and Colman arrived at an inspired moment with fresh beef. Jesus taught his disciples that "Where God guides, He provides." It is the normal miraculous working of the economics of unselfishness by which He Himself lived. Nothing could have interested the Roman priests more.

The Romans had brought with them the gift of a gold pectoral cross from Gregory for Columcille. In gratitude the abbot wrote his finest Latin poem, *Altus Prosator*:

> . . . From the fruitful breast of Heaven,
> While changing seasons wax and wane,
> The welcome streams that never fail
> Pour forth in rich supplies of grain . . .

When Pope Gregory received the poem, he wrote back warmly praising it and sending some hymns to Columcille.

The gold pectoral cross was treasured at Iona and then, for greater safety, at the Columban monastery on Tory Island off the north Irish coast. Later it came into the keeping of the MacDonnells of Dunluce in Ulster. During the Elizabethan Wars Dunluce was stormed and looted in 1584. Sir John Perrot, Deputy of Ireland, took the cross and sent it to a lady friend in London with a facetious note. The note survives in the State Papers but the fate of Columcille's cross is unknown.

* * *

Throughout the Middle Ages it was believed in Scotland that St. Mungo went to Rome about 590 and met

St. Gregory. The outcome of this visit was the mission to the English led by St. Augustine in 596. This belief was supported by the evidence of Mungo's Bell and, as reported by Adomnan, the visit of the papal delegation to Iona early in the 590s, bringing the Pope's gift of a pectoral cross to Columcille.

This evidence appears to lead to the conclusion that these great men of God — Mungo of Glasgow, Columcille of Iona, Pope Gregory and Augustine of Canterbury — worked as a united team to win the English for God's glory. What set this action in motion was Mungo's journey to Rome.

Chapter twenty-seven

Having destroyed the work of King Urien, the pagan princes who reigned in Edinburgh decided to do it over again: they sent out a call across Britain for volunteers to recapture Catterick.

They came from as far away as Cornwall, high-spirited young horsemen in a knight-errant mood. The commander, Mynydawc of Edinburgh, called up all the fighting men of the Votadini tribe to provide the infantry. Arthur's cavalry had been fast and formidable because it was well mounted but, since his day, the Britons had neglected horse-breeding and their horses were of poor quality.

The English had found a gifted commander, Ethelfrith of Bernicia. The English usually chose to fight in the open, but at Catterick Ethelfrith placed his men behind the protection of the ancient Roman walls. Again, Arthur would never have launched cavalry against stone fortifications. Mynydawc did — and watched his cavalry destroyed. Then his unprotected infantry was hunted down. That day the Votadini ceased to exist as a tribe.

Aneiran the bard tells the story in his poem *Gododdin*:

> The men went to Catterick in the dawn
> Shouting for battle,
> A squadron of horse,
> Pale mead was their feast.
> And it was their poison . . .
> Blue their armour and shields,
> Sharp lances uplifted,
> Mail and sword glinting.
> After the wine they left us.
> I know the sorrow of their death.
> They were slain, they never grew grey.

Columcille's writing table

*"In veneration will this island be held, not only by the
Scots but by holy men of other churches"*

The Cloridderick Stone

The tomb of St. Mungo in the Under Church of Glasgow Cathedral

From the army of Mynydawc,
Of three hundred men, only one returned.

* * *

A conflict with a rather different result had taken place in the south. The small Welsh kingdom of Glevissig, now Glamorgan, had been ruled by the abbot-king Cadoc. When he felt that age was beginning to reduce his capability, he resigned the throne and retired into his monastery of Llancarfan.

He had long since chosen his successor and had tutored him to assume the government — a devout, gifted young man named Mouric. His grandfather had commanded the Britons' fleet in Arthur's time. Mouric's mother was Enhinti, sister of King Urien, and his father was Theodoric, who had been king in Brittany but who had given it up to become a monk and hermit at Tintern on the River Wye.

To the east of Glevissig lay the English kingdom of the conquering Ceawlin, who had routed the Britons in 577 at Dyrham near Bath and had carried English conquest to the River Severn and the Bristol Channel. He was now casting covetous eyes at the rich agricultural lands of South Wales. In 584 he attacked with a strong English force, intending to cross the Wye by Tintern Ford. Warned by an angel, Theodoric left his cell, rallied the British warriors and took command. The English attacks were decisively repulsed and Ceawlin, so tradition says, "returned home in anger." No English warrior dared to cross the River Wye for centuries, but Theodoric fell at Tintern Ford, mortally wounded.

Across the Wye from the Britons of Glevissig lived an English tribe, the Hwicces. The victory at the ford opened the way for Cadoc's monks from Llancarfan to reach out in friendship to the Hwicces. Soon the water of the beautiful River Wye was used to baptize erstwhile enemies whom the monks now claimed as friends. The tribe of the Hwicces became almost completely Christian. Although they were part of the larger pagan kingdom of Mercia, the Hwicces were not harassed even when the overlord was the aggressive heathen Penda. The Hwicces and the Britons often fought as allies but never attacked each other.

Cadoc's monks and townspeople had demonstrated that the Christian Welsh could win the English to Christ if they tried. Even today, the title of the Bishop of Worcester describes him as "Episcopus Hwicciorum."

Chapter twenty-eight

Columcille walked slowly on Iona in the June sunshine, helped by his devoted servant Diarmid. At 77 years of age, he was frail. He sat on the grassy bank to rest and the old white pony that pulled the milk cart came up and nuzzled against him. "Somehow God has let him know that his master is going to leave him," said the abbot. Diarmid was distressed that Columcille talked of dying. "Today is the Sabbath," the abbot went on, "when I rest from my labours. Jesus has invited me and at midnight I shall go to our fathers." Then he climbed up to his cell on Tor Abb and, with the disciplined habit of a lifetime, sat at his desk and wrote a passage of Scripture, Psalm 34: "They that seek the Lord shall not want for any good thing." Then he laid down his quill.

Word spread rapidly throughout the island that the abbot was not well and the brothers came running to gather around him. Gazing across the island, straits and ocean to the mountains of Mull, he foretold: "In veneration will this island be held, not only by the Scots but by holy men of other churches. Have true love between each other and God will give you not only your needs but eternal gifts as well."

The abbey bell rang in the dark, heralding the Lord's Day. The old man hurried down to the church, outdistancing all the rest. When the brothers arrived with torches they found Columcille lying before the altar, arms outstretched, his luminous grey eyes bright with joy. He looked from man to man, signing each with his blessing. So passed a prince who had traded the sceptre of Ireland for a pilgrim's staff. He was the "rich young ruler" who said "Yes" to Christ, choosing to own nothing, to share with the hungry, to set free the slave, to find peace in forgiveness and to befriend enemies. He became the model and hero of the Gael and stands forth as Ireland's greatest son and the founding father of the Scottish race.

To Rydderch, Mungo and the citizens of Glasgow, Columcille's passing was like a death in the family. For so long their lives had interlocked. He had been their *amn chara*. Yet their hearts overflowed with gratitude and glory. It was a time for singing the songs he had loved, so many of which he had himself written.

*   *   *

A couple of months later news reached Mungo, thrilling news for which he and Columcille had worked and prayed. Roman priests had landed in England. Led by Augustine, Prior of St. Andrew's, they had landed in Kent and been received, rather cautiously at first, by Ethelbert, Bretwalda (over-king) of England. He had housed them in his capital of Canterbury and granted them permission to preach. The old Roman chapel of St. Martin was theirs for services and Queen Bertha, who was a Christian and had brought her chaplain with her from Paris, joined in their worship.

Pope Gregory had never wavered in his determination to reach out to the English. In spite of being bedridden with fevers and crippled by gout and having to contend with the dual threats of plague within Rome and heretics without, he kept true to his purpose. Finally in 596 he had been able to dispatch three dozen of his men from St. Andrew's. But when the missionaries reached Gaul, they heard such stories of English savagery that it had unnerved them and Augustine had gone back to Rome to entreat Gregory to recall them. These were brave men, as their lives were to prove, but the dangers were such as to daunt even them.

Gregory had written back to them: "Gregory, servant of the servants of God: it is better never to undertake a high enterprise than to abandon it once begun. Do not be deterred by what men say. The greater the labour, the greater will be the glory. God keep you safe, my dearest sons." Yet he may have wondered if he was sending them to their death. But five years later came the news that King Ethelbert had been baptized and 10,000 of his people had followed his example.

In 603 Augustine, the first Archbishop of Canterbury, took a daring journey to the west. Though he was terminally ill, he went to meet the Celtic bishops. At Aust on the River Severn he met two bishops and the abbot and monks of the monastery of Bangor-is-coed. But his request for their help to win the English for Christ was rejected. It matters little whose fault it was. The chance went past for ever. How eagerly Cadoc, David and Iltud would have grasped it! But they were dead. Before he returned to Kent, Augustine spoke a word of warning: "If you do not preach the Gospel to the English, you will suffer death at their hands."

Augustine died the next year. He had done in England what Gregory had sent him to do. Canterbury is his abiding memorial. That same year, Pope Gregory wrote joyfully: "The tongues of the English have begun to cry Alleluia!" On his tomb in St. Peter's in Rome are carved the words:

TO CHRIST HE LED THE ENGLISH
BY GOD'S GRACE
SWELLING FAITH'S ARMIES
WITH A NEW WON RACE

Chapter twenty-nine

There was a new power in Britain. Bernicia under Ethelfrith, victor of Catterick, was a force to be reckoned with. He was a soldier's soldier, with original ideas, an eye for the weak spot and a fine sense of timing. At Catterick he held the door to Scotland. The Britons themselves had destroyed Reged, the one kingdom which might have curbed him. If he crushed Strathclyde his control would stretch from the Firth of Forth to the Firth of Clyde.

Ethelfrith marched his Bernicians up the Teviot to the head of Liddesdale where, at Dawstane, his path was barred by the Britons and their allies. On their right were the Ulster Irish and on the left the Dalriada Scots. The army was under the command of Aidan, king of the Scots, who had been granted the title of ''Guletic,'' the title Arthur had borne.

The Irish charge broke the opposing English, but on the left the Scots were driven back. Aidan's son Domangart struggled to re-form the line but, when he was cut down, there was a rout. A hundred years later the Venerable Bede wrote: ''From this time forth no King of Scots ventured to come in battle against the English.''

Aidan was shattered by the defeat. He never got over it. He resigned his command and returned to Dalriada. There, he abdicated in favour of his youngest son Eochaid Buidhe and ''retired into religion.'' He died about 606 AD, feeling his life had been a failure.

Though Aidan never knew it, his life was a catalyst for the emergence of a new Scottish nation. He was the son of a Gaelic father and a British mother, the grandson of a Saxon princess. He married the Princess Royal of

the Picts and their marriage was the event which termi-
nated the enmity between Pict and Scot. Their son became
the High King of the Picts. Aidan worked in close friendship with the greatest men of the age to establish the
Christian faith so firmly in the north that it has never
since been shaken. He was the first king in Britain to
receive Christian consecration, and in the twentieth century "by the Grace of God" his descendants sit upon the
throne of Great Britain.

Aidan's old friend Rydderch of Alclyde had also passed
away, dying in his own bed "with [your] head on a
feather pillow," as Columcille had foretold. He is buried
beside a massive rock at the head of Lochwinnoch,
15 miles west of Glasgow. The rock is called Cloridderick,
which the local people pronounce "Cloth-rick," giving
the double "d" in the name the "th" sound it would
have in Welsh.

Through exile, warfare, treachery and triumph this
courageous and constant man kept the faith, a Roman
Briton whom the British of today should hold in honour.

* * *

The little bronze bell, the gift of Pope Gregory, tinkled
in the candlelit dusk of Glasgow's abbey church. Mungo's
voice saying Mass was indistinct because of the bandage
he wore over his head and under his chin. He was very
old now and the muscles of his jaw were so weak that
he could not close his mouth. Physicians think that this
was the result of a form of muscular dystrophy. Yet in
spite of these infirmities, the happy radiance of his spirit

A replica (actual size) of Mungo's Bell (by permission of the People's Palace, Glasgow Museums)

touched everyone in the community. He was still the Beloved.

On Sunday January 13, 603 AD, Mungo felt a keen desire for a hot bath. This is not an unusual desire of those who are terminally ill and in palliative care hospitals today special baths are available. Also, as mentioned earlier, throughout his life Mungo had followed the Roman tradition of the daily hot bath. It is noteworthy that there was a bath at his abbey, possibly salvaged at his request from the bathhouse of an abandoned Roman fort.

With affectionate care his "Eglais Cu" prepared the bath and the monks carried the old bishop and gently lowered him into the warm soothing water. After a time he rallied and, with a last effort, spoke: "My children . . . love one another . . . be hospitable . . . beware of heresy . . . keep the laws of the Church . . . she is the Mother of us all." His jaw dropped and the soul of the Beloved was gone.

His brethren laid him to rest beneath the altar in the little wooden abbey church beside the Molindinar Burn and his people made pilgrimage to pray beside him. Nearly 600 years later a splendid stone cathedral was built around his tomb, where he lies today.

But Mungo could know nothing of that. He, Rydderch and Aidan each died under the shadow of failure. They had once seen Christianity almost wiped out in Britain; they had suffered persecution and exile but had fought back. Now it seemed about to happen again. Ethelfrith's pagan army stood on the threshold of Scotland and there was nothing to stop him.

How many of the saints have died in apparent failure! Peter and Paul died while their flock was massacred in Rome. Calvary itself seemed like total failure.

> Yet behind the dim unknown
> Standeth God within the shadow
> Keeping watch above His own.

Chapter thirty

Mungo's story did not end when death closed his eyes. To understand the growth of Britain we must not forget his abiding, formative influence and that of his great friend, Columcille of Iona. With this in mind, let us follow Scotland's story.

* * *

Ethelfrith never in fact unleashed his army on Strathclyde and the dreaded shadow passed harmlessly by, because the conqueror was tempted by more attractive targets further south. Based in the lands of Deira around York, which he had annexed in 604, he could strike at Chester, reach the Irish Sea and cut off the Britons of Wales from their kinsmen, the North Britons.

In 616 Ethelfrith marched on Chester and the Britons of Wales massed all their manpower to defend it. They also mobilized their prayer-power, and nearly 2,000 monks from the monastery of Bangor-is-coed gathered on a hill near the battlelines and filled the air with their imprecations and psalms.

Ethelfrith studied them, then asked what they were doing. When told they were praying, he remarked grimly: "If they are praying against us, they are fighting against us." He launched his first attack straight at the clerics. Twelve hundred of them died in the massacre. The warriors of the Britons were so shaken to see their "men of religion" slaughtered that they broke ranks and fled. Augustine's warning had gone unheeded.

The victor of Catterick, Dawstane and Chester, the unchallenged master of Britain, at the height of his power, now made a fatal error. Like most pagan kings, Ethelfrith lived in fear of a rival. He dreaded his brother-in-law Edwin, son of Aelle, king of Deira. He had chased Edwin into exile and had used paid assassins to hound him from one refuge to another. Edwin was at that time living precariously among the East Saxons.

After the victory at Chester, Ethelfrith's soldiers were laden with booty and he thought it would be no great risk to let them go home for a short rest. Edwin saw his chance. Scraping together a small striking force, he caught his enemy almost unguarded at the River Idle and killed him. Edwin, one day a hunted fugitive, the next became the most powerful of English kings!

Edwin marched to York and the people of Deira, his father's kingdom, rallied to him. Then he pressed on into Bernicia, Ethelfrith's home territory, and there the people proclaimed him king. He marched on into the Lothians and captured the great rock of Dunedin — and changed its name to Edinburgh.

His life had never been safe enough for him to consider marriage. Now he turned to his kinsman, the king of Kent. King Eadbald agreed to Edwin's marriage with his sister, Princess Ethelberga, but only on condition that she could take Christian servants and a chaplain with her and practise her faith. Edwin at once agreed. In his unhappy wanderings he had met some Christians who had rather impressed him.

Ethelberga, nicknamed Tata, was the daughter of Queen Bertha, who herself had come as a Christian bride to a pagan court, and therefore Tata was not ignorant of how much would depend on the way she lived. Edwin and his wife went north to the kingdom which was becoming known as Northumbria. As her chaplain the queen took Bishop Paulinus, a man trained by Gregory and sent to Britain in 601 to give Augustine extra support. He was tall and dark, with a hawk-like nose and an awe-inspiring presence.

Yet, the most astonishing part of the unexpected turn of events that had occurred in Britain over the period of a year or so was taking place far away in Scotland. When King Ethelfrith fell, his sons had to run for their lives. In 617 the two orphaned lads arrived on the island of Iona asking for sanctuary. Abbot Fergna Brit took them in, as the brethren did with hundreds of waifs, regardless of race, speech or belief. They made them welcome, gave them a home, an education and a faith. Oswald, the older boy, was about 13 years old, his little brother, Oswy, only five.

Chapter thirty-one

In his royal hall of Deira near York King Edwin was holding high holiday. He had just announced the joyful news
that his wife Tata had given birth to their first child, a
daughter Eanfled. Among the noisy well-wishers crowd-
ing around him with uplifted drinking horns was a stealthy
assassin who lunged at him with a poisoned dagger. The
royal counsellor Lilla saw the glint of a knife in time to
hurl himself forward and take the blade in his own body.

Grieving for the death of his loyal friend, yet grateful
for his own escape, Edwin went up to see his wife and
baby. Together they thanked God and, deeply moved,
the king promised Tata that their little Eanfled should be
dedicated to Christ. It was Easter Sunday in the year 626.

Edwin was a deep thinker, given to long periods alone
pondering in his heart the right decisions to take. After
this experience he was convinced that the time had come
to place the issue of acceptance of the new faith before
his council, the Witanagemot. He convened it at
Goodmanham.

A respected earlderman spoke first. "Man does not
know where he came from or where he is going. We are
like a bird flying out of the dark into this brightly lit hall
for a moment, then out into the dark again. If this new
doctrine can teach us something about life's mystery, we
should receive it."

But the great surprise of the council was the speech
of Coifi, the pagan High Priest. "I have long realized that
there is nothing in our worship. The more I sought for
truth, the less I found. None has been more devout than
I and if our gods had power, surely they would have
favoured me, but others got greater honours. But this

new teaching reveals truth that gives blessing in this life
and eternal happiness. Our altars are of no use and should
be burned. I will do it myself.''

Pagan priests were prohibited from carrying weapons
or riding a war horse, but Coifi borrowed a stallion, a
sword and spears from the king and galloped away to
the pagan temple. There, he hurled the spears, breaking
the idols, while an astonished crowd watched, quite sure
he had gone mad.

On Easter Day 627 Edwin and his nobles came to York
where, in the little log and thatch church of St. Peter,
they were baptized by Bishop Paulinus. All that summer
Bishop Paulinus baptized the English, first at Yeavering
beside the River Glen, then at Catterick on the River Swale.
They came in their thousands, in families, men, women
and children, wading into the shining water at the ford.
Paulinus did not work alone. The British Bishop Rhun
came to help him. Rhun was a grandson of Urien and
therefore a cousin of St. Mungo, whose successor he was
as bishop of Cumbria. Here was one Briton who gave
himself heart and soul to preach the Gospel to the English.
At Catterick the flower of Britain's youth had fallen in
battle. What more fitting place for a Roman and a Briton
to baptize former foes into the family of heaven? As
Gregory had said, ''Aelle's son and all his people are
singing Alleluia!''

For six years the promise of a new age spread throughout Northumbria. Edwin made the roads safe for travel.
It was said that, in his day, a mother carrying her baby
could walk in safety from sea to sea. The king placed
bronze cups at all the springs along the roads for the use
of travellers, and they were never stolen.

But not everyone was pleased by the changes taking place in Northumbria. A neighbouring king, Penda of Mercia, was bitterly anti-Christian. When he caught some of his subjects preaching the Gospel, he buried them all under a huge pile of stones at a place still called Stone. Edwin's actions infuriated him. He found a somewhat strange ally in Cadwallon, king of Gwynedd, a nominal Christian. Though there were no doubt disagreements as to the excuse for war, the real motive of these odd allies seemed to be malice.

In 633 they attacked and brought Edwin to battle at Hatfield, just south of York. He was defeated and killed. The victors spread fire and sword savagely throughout the kingdom, swearing to destroy Northumbria utterly. Bishop Paulinus hurried the widowed Queen Tata and her small daughter away by sea to the safety of Kent.

Chapter thirty-two

In the creative atmosphere of Iona, Oswald, the young Englishman, grew and matured until, in the words of Bede, he became "a man beloved of God." When he was 25 years old, news came that his uncle, King Edwin, and thousands of his people in Northumbria had been baptized. He was 31 when he heard the shocking news that Penda and Cadwallon had killed Edwin and were trying to blot out Christianity in Northumbria by wholesale slaughter.

It was not for Oswald to take action, as he was not the heir. His older brother Eanfrith was living among the Picts. However, while trying to negotiate a peace with Cadwallon, he was murdered.

Oswald, the monk kneeling before Iona's altar, now faced the challenge of his life. He felt strongly that it was his duty to rescue his suffering fellow-countrymen from brutal tyranny and continue the work of conversion. From among refugees and exiles in the north he recruited a small fighting force and, with the Cross as his standard, led them into Northumbria.

The members of Cadwallon's veteran army far outnumbered those of Oswald's small brigade, but they were booty-glutted and carelessly posted. That night Oswald had a vivid dream of Columcille encouraging him. When he awoke, he decided to attempt the most risky of military tactics — a night attack. But first, as Mungo had been wont to do, he raised a large wooden Cross.

The night attack was a complete surprise, creating panic and rout. The invaders fled in terror and Cadwallon was ridden down and slain. The battle was named Heavenfield. Bernicia and Deira both rallied to Oswald, proclaiming him king, and he was soon acknowledged as Bretwalda of all England. He asked to receive his consecration in the same manner as King Aidan had received it from Columcille at Iona.

Oswald's renown was to become great and abiding in the affections of the English people. Only Alfred the Great is held in such high regard. Bede thus explained the secret of his hold on his people's affections: "Although he reached such a height of power, Oswald was always humble, kindly and generous to the poor and strangers." His first act was to request the abbot of Iona to send a bishop to teach his English folk the Christian way. The man who was sent was Bishop Corman. He was a serious, devout, clever man, but he put the truth too far above the heads of his listeners. He touched no hearts. Before long he gave up and retreated to Iona, complaining that the English were obstinate and quite ungovernable.

While the brethren were discussing his report, a Scot named Aidan gently suggested: "Maybe our Brother was too severe. Why not begin with the milk of simple teaching, as the Apostles did, and afterwards feed them with the loftier precepts?" The eyes of all the assembly turned and looked at Aidan. It was not long before he was consecrated bishop and was on his way to Northumbria.

If anyone may be called the spiritual heir of Columcille, it is Aidan. He had the same gentle strength, the same kindness of a God-given love. From the very first contact he thawed the stubborn hearts of the English. Bede, himself an Englishman, wrote:

> I admire and love all these things about Aidan. On his arrival King Oswald gave Aidan the island of Lindisfarne

near his capital of Bamburgh. As the tide ebbs and flows, twice a day, Lindisfarne becomes an island.

The King listened readily to Aidan and together they set about establishing the Church throughout the Kingdom. Aidan was not yet fluent in English and it was delightful to see the King interpreting for his thanes, for he spoke Gaelic perfectly.

Aidan gave his clergy an inspiring example of self-discipline and continence. The highest recommendation of his teaching was that he and his followers lived as they taught. He never sought or cared for earthly possessions but loved to give to the poor whatever wealthy folk gave him.

He travelled on foot in town or country, stopping to talk to anyone, high or low, pagan or Christian. He expected all who walked with him to meditate and read Scripture.

When invited by the King to dinner, he brought along a couple of clergy, ate sparingly and left as soon as possible. If wealthy people did wrong, he would not keep silent out of respect or fear, but corrected them outspokenly. If rich men gave him money he used it to ransom slaves, many of whom later became priests.

King and bishop, Oswald and Aidan — how the stories must have gone the rounds, more amazing than the sagas of old. A favourite tale that has lasted down the centuries is about an Easter feast. Oswald and the bishop had just sat down to dine. A rich meal was laid before them, served on a silver dish. At that moment, the almoner approached and told the king that there was a crowd of needy people sitting in the road outside the palace. At once Oswald commanded that the meal be taken out and shared among the people and the silver platter be broken up into pieces and distributed among them. Aidan, deeply moved, took the king's right hand, saying, ''May this hand never wither!''

Lindisfarne had grown into ''a second Iona among the English.'' Bede gave this picture of it:

> There were few buildings except the church. Indeed no more than met the need of a seemly way of life. The monks had no property except cattle and gave to the poor any money they received. They had no need of money to provide lodging for important people. Those who visited came only to pray and hear the word of God. If they stayed for a meal they were content with the plain food of the Brothers. The religious dress was therefore held in high esteem. A priest came to a village solely to baptize, visit the sick and care for souls.

There was also a great effort at this time to improve relations between north and south. Oswald received news that Pope Honorius had sent Bishop Birinus to the Saxons in the Thames Valley. When their king Cynegils requested baptism, he asked Oswald to be his godfather. Later, Cynegils' daughter married Oswald. This is one of many examples of cordial cooperation between Celts and Romans.

Chapter thirty-three

Oswald was the pride and boast of his people, a kind of king the English had never known before. But he shared the British Isles with many kings of the old type, who lived by fear and the drawn sword. Oswald's popularity enraged them. Most of all it infuriated the envious Penda of Mercia. In 642 he saw his chance to force Oswald to battle and they fought at Oswestry. Oswald died, calling on God as he fell to forgive his enemies.

Penda reverted to a barbarism most of the English had abandoned. He mutilated the body of the dead king, hacking off the head and hands and nailing them to a tree. In Oswestry the tale is told that an eagle swooped down, tore loose the right hand and flew away with it. Where the bird dropped it, a spring came up which was a ''healing well.'' It still flows. Oswald's head was later placed in the tomb of St. Cuthbert in Durham Cathedral.

Oswald dead proved to be as potent a force as when he was alive. He became a folk hero and an inspiration to all the English, a standard by which they judged other kings. His younger brother Oswy, as an Iona-trained Christian, was cordially accepted as king of Northumbria. He had married Reinmelth of the royal house of Urien and, through her inheritance of the royal title of Cumbria, had become the ruler of Cumbria. Reinmelth was also a great-niece of Bishop Rhun who in 627 had worked with Paulinus to baptize the English of Northumbria. Oswy and his wife had a son Alchfrid, to whom they gave the finest education at Iona.

Alchfrid became a man of distinguished scholarship, one of the most learned of the age, a friend of Aldhelm of Malmesbury and Adomnan of Iona. But, although interested in books, he was more interested in the lives of men. He made a special effort to become friends with Prince Peada, son and heir of Penda of Mercia. When Alchfrid met Cyniburg, Peada's sister, they fell in love and married.

Peada was a worthy prince, at that time ruling the Middle Saxons near London. He wanted to marry Alchfleda, Alchfrid's sister. He gathered together his thanes and set out for Bamburgh to ask King Oswy for his daughter's hand. But Oswy refused unless Peada was first baptized. Peada had questioned Alchfrid closely about his faith and now he unhesitatingly answered: "I will gladly become a Christian, even if the Princess refuses me." He and all his thanes were thereupon baptized.

When Peada returned to Mercia he took with him four priests: Chedd, Adda and Betti from Lindisfarne, and Diuma, a Scot from Iona. At Sandbach, a town near Crewe, they held a great assembly at which Peada publicly made known to his people why he had chosen the Christian way. Even Penda his father, though he grumbled, no longer forbade the preaching of the Gospel in Mercia. In Sandbach still stand the two splendid stone crosses that commemorate Prince Peada's mission.

This had all occurred about 650, but by 655 Penda had reverted to his old ways. He mobilized a huge army to crush Oswy and the Northumbrians. Oswy, hoping to buy him off, "offered an incalculable quantity of regalia." But the bitter Penda refused, vowing to wipe out the Northumbrians to a man. In these straits Oswy declared: "If the heathen refuse our gifts, let us offer them to the Lord."

He and Alchfrid mustered what troops they could but, when the armies faced each other near Leeds, Penda's

host was thirty times larger than Oswy's. But the valley of the River Winwaed where they met was marshy and flooded. The grey Yorkshire skies rained torrents. There was no firm ground for manoeuvre. Floundering in the mud, old Penda lost his army and his life.

* * *

Three years later Oswy died peacefully in his bed, something few of his ancestors had managed. He was not the beloved saint his brother had been, but he was a good man who grew better. He played a worthy part in bringing the faith to England.

It was just a century since Mungo had built his missionary training base at Llanelwy, a century since Columcille had stepped ashore on Iona to relight the fire of faith in the heathen darkness of Britain. Only a century. And now the light of that fire shone from the foot of Cornwall to the craggy cliffs of Cape Wrath in the far north, and it was an Englishman, Deusdedit, who sat in the archbishop's Chair at Canterbury. Picts, Scots, Welsh and English all lived under the rule of Christian kings.

Alchfrid ruled Cumbria until 685 and then became king of all Northumbria for 20 years. He applied his scholarship and skill to developing the art and literature of the north. There was an explosion of artistic genius, hitherto unsuspected, among the diverse people of England — the Lindisfarne Gospel; the poems of Caedmon, the ploughman poet; the *History* and other writings of Bede. Such a literary flowering does not just happen; there has to be a spark that lights the blaze. It is possible that the brilliant Alchfrid provided that spark.

The Northumbrian stone carving which also flourished shows the influence of both Rome and Ireland, but it was a new and unique artistry. One of the most famous examples is the Ruthwell Cross. It was created to replace the wooden "preaching cross" raised by St. Mungo there during the great assembly at Hoddam a century earlier. It seems very likely that the idea to replace the wooden Cross came from Alchfrid. Mungo was the Cumbrians' very own saint. Alchfrid, through his mother, was a kinsman of the saint and he may have thought it his filial duty to replace the Cross with a memorial of surpassing beauty.

The Ruthwell Cross remains today pre-eminent in the elaboration of its scenes and the splendour of its vine scroll. Upon the Cross are some lines from the most moving and original of Anglo-Saxon poems, *The Dream of the Rood*. The Cross tells its own story from the time it was a tree in the forest until, after bearing aloft the Lord of Heaven, it was buried deep in a pit, thereafter to become the symbol of Creation:

> Was I there with blood bedabbled,
> Gushing grievous from His side
> When His ghost He had up-rendered? . . .

The circumstances that produced the Ruthwell Cross had also altered the course of English history. The sudden change from barbaric devastation to creative artistry, from a pagan Penda to a learned Alchfrid, is the most remarkable transformation of that age.

The Ruthwell Cross stands like a superb war memorial, commemorating victory in the most crucial struggle the British ever fought in the war of faith.

RUTHWELL

Fragment
from the
churchyard

* * *

How then to end this story that has no ending? The story of Mungo's victory lives on in every generation and is inherent in our blood.

Since Mungo's day the British have thought of themselves as a Christian nation. Mungo is a worthy role-model for today's leaders of Church and State who must face the present-day threats in the war of faith.

In every age it is always the few who dare to do the nigh-impossible *because it has to be done*. The battle Mungo fought and the victory he won are the inheritance of our race.

The stone crosses at Sandbach, Cheshire

The Rev. R. M. Neil, minister of Ruthwell, standing beside the Ruthwell Cross

Notes

Page

xix. The baptismal name of Columcille, a prince of the Royal line of the Ui Neill, was Colum but his devotion to the Church as a young man earned him the nickname ''Columcille'' (''dove of the Church''). The Irish still call him that. When his story was written later in Latin, he was called Columba. In this book it seems fitting to use his Gaelic name.

3. The standard of a Roman legion (division) was an Eagle. The standard of a Roman cohort (regiment) was a Dragon and the army commander or king came to be called ''The Dragon'' (cf. ''The Island Dragon,'' p. 49). Cohorts were identified by colours. The Votadini bore a Red Dragon standard and marched behind it when Cunedda led them to North Wales at the beginning of the fourth century to drive the Irish invaders out of Anglesey. Thus Wales got its Red Dragon. The Strathclyde cohort bore a Green Dragon standard and for hundreds of years the men of Strathclyde were called ''The Britons of the Green Standard.''

8. The name ''Tannoc'' may be derived from ''Tannith,'' the feminine personification of the Sun God. The ending -oc is a diminutive denoting affection. The name appears in many forms: Taneu, Thaney, Dwynwen, Enoch.

Symbol of Tannith

13.   During excavations at Traprain Law iron tyres of the
      wheels of a small cart were found, implying that small
      carts were used at Dunpelder.

16.   The site of Mungo's birth seems always to have been
      marked in early times by some memorial on the beach
      at Culross, each replaced by a new one when it became
      dilapidated. The present shrine was built by Archbishop
      Blackader of Glasgow in 1503.

21.   During excavation of the hill fort on Traprain Law in
      1919, a cache of Roman silver was uncovered, the richest
      hoard ever found in Scotland: 100 silver plates, 50 bowls,
      10 flagons. Coins showed that it was hidden after the
      reign of Honorius (d. 423). The silver had been cut and
      flattened for melting. Many items bore Christian motifs,
      biblical scenes and the Chi-Rho monogram.

26.   The name "Glasgow" has been mistakenly said to derive
      from two Gaelic words: Glas cu ("blue dog"). But Gaelic
      was not spoken in this area until long after the city was
      founded.

38.   The raising of the great "preaching cross" at Crosthwaite
      seems to have started a practice in Britain that survives
      to this day. Mungo himself often raised "preaching
      crosses" — at Hoddam, at Glasgow and elsewhere. The
      market cross in the centre of mediaeval towns, such as
      Banbury Cross and Charing Cross, was a derivation of
      this practice. Memorial crosses like the Martyrs' Memorial
      in Oxford led naturally to war memorial crosses.

42.   When Germanus arrived in 420, Britain was being
      harassed by war-bands of Picts and Saxons. The British
      troops were demoralized. During the winter of 429,
      Germanus re-formed, drilled and inspired them in his
      camp near Mold, Wales. When the invaders attacked in
      the Spring the Britons were ready. Germanus drew up
      a company of his troops in full view at the head of the

valley, but concealed other companies on either flank. The raiders, contemptuous of the Britons' courage, charged wildly up the valley. At a signal the flank companies sprang up, shouting "Alleluia!" The enemy panicked and ran, many drowning in the flooded River Alyn.

52. There were three serious outbreaks of yellow plague in Britain during the sixth century — 548, 558 and 563. Because the plague first broke out in 548, several histories give this as the date of Maelgwn's death. But had he died in 548, Maelgwn could never have met Mungo who at that date was still in Scotland. Had he died in the outbreak of 563, Maelgwn would still have been king of Gwynedd when his pagan son-in-law, Elifer, attacked Caernarfon in 560; but his son Rhun was already king by then. It therefore appears that Maelgwn died in the outbreak of 558.

63. There are two stories illustrating Columcille's dealings with the Druids, who were less welcoming than Brude. In fact the Arch Druid Broichan and his fellow sages viewed the abbots with cold hostility. Broichan was Brude's foster father, his tutor and now his chief advisor. These Scots were a threat to all he stood for. One evening the abbots were quietly singing Vespers together when the Druids raised a deafening racket. Columcille's glorious singing voice could, if needed, rise with the power of a trumpet. That evening at full volume he sang Psalm 45: "My tongue is the pen of a ready writer." Friend and foe alike were hushed with awe.

   By the time the abbots were ready to start their journey home, the Arch Druid had worked himself into a nervous state and was sure he was dying. Brude appealed to Columcille to save his foster father's life. Columcille did two things. Firstly, he found a white stone that floated — possibly pumice — and sent it to Broichan, telling him to put it in water, then drink the water. Secondly, he told Broichan to set free a Gaelic girl whom he held captive.

Obedience, the first step in anyone's transformation, was to be followed by moral change. Broichan obeyed and recovered his health, the girl went free and the Druid became a devoted friend of Columcille.

63. Adomnan, born in Ireland in 624, was renowned as a scholar and was abbot of Iona from 679 to 704. Adomnan is said to have written several books but only two are definitely known to be by him. One of these is his biography of Columcille, *Vita S. Columbae*.

69. A living link with that great gathering at Hoddam is the family of Carruthers which is descended from the Hereditary Castellans of the Royal Castle of Hoddam, hence their name CAER RYDDERCH ("Carruthers"). The family members must have been kinsmen of the great king, for no Celtic ruler would trust his protection to men not of his own blood.

In the thirteenth century, when the first written record of the family occurs, they are described as "Hereditary Rectors of Ruthwell" where stands the wonderfully carved Cross, raised as a memorial to Mungo's preaching mission at Hoddam. The village of Carrutherstown is only two miles away.

The family's reputation as trusty castellans was so high that, when the Norman family of Bruce built the castle of Lochmaben, they asked the Carruthers to take charge of it. The families intermarried and today the Carruthers are a Sept of Clan Bruce.

87. "Mungo's Bell" seems to have survived in use at Glasgow Cathedral throughout the Middle Ages. It was used at altar services and for "the repose of the souls of the dead." After the spoilation of the Cathedral during the Reformation, the bell fell into the hands of a citizen,

Andrew Lang, who in 1577 ''brought to the Baillie and Council the old Bell and was created a Burgess gratis.'' The bell was still in use in Glasgow in 1631 and is recorded as being in existence as late as 1661.

Chronology

c. 540   St. Finnian taught the "Twelve Apostles of Ireland" at Clonard.

c. 545   Pagan resurgence in northern Britain. Gwendoleu seized Carlisle. Bishop of Falkirk martyred, Whithorn sacked.

          Kentigern became priest of church at Cathures (Glasgow).

c. 550   Kentigern ordained bishop at age of 25. Driven into exile by pagans. Escaped to Cumbria.

550-53   Kentigern preaching at the wells in Cumbria. Convened great assembly at Crosthwaite in 553.

          Kentigern travelled to North Wales in 553 and met King Cadwallon and his uncle St. Asaph.

          Kentigern and Asaph confronted the great King Maelgwn and cured his blindness.

c. 555   Kentigern and Asaph founded monastery of Llanelwy in North Wales.

          King Elifer attacked Caernarfon, was defeated by Maelgwn's son, King Rhun, and killed on the beach.

558   Maelgwn died of the yellow plague.

561   Battle of Culdremne. Irish Druid army defeated by Christian tribes of Northwest Ireland.

c. 561-62 Rhun's Long March without bloodshed, through Cumbria and the north, demonstrated the power of Gwynedd.

563   Columcille founded monastery on Iona.

565   Columcille, Comgall and Kenneth journeyed to Inverness. High King Brude MacMaelchon converted.

573	Battle of Arthuret. Kentigern recalled to Strathclyde by King Rydderch.
574	Aidan consecrated King of Scots at Iona by Columcille.
	Kentigern and King Rydderch conducted great mission assembly at Hoddam in Strathclyde.
580	Adda of Bernicia defeated and killed Peredur of York at Caergreu. York fell.
581-82	Kentigern returned to Glasgow.
584	Brude MacMaelchon killed at battle of Circenn.
585	King Aidan defeated Maeatae Picts and Saxons at battle of Dumyat.
	Combined missionary campaign launched from Dunkeld to convert southern Picts. St. Kenneth founded Kilrymont (St. Andrews).
590	Kentigern went to Rome to visit Pope Gregory. Pope sent seven emissaries to Iona to visit Columcille.
596-97	St. Augustine landed in Kent with 40 missionaries sent by Pope Gregory. Granted a church at Canterbury by King Ethelbert of Kent.
597	Death of Columcille at Iona.
603	Death of Rydderch and St. Kentigern.
604	Death of Pope Gregory and St. Augustine.
	Battle of Dawstane. King Aidan, Scots and Britons defeated by King Ethelfrith of Northumbria.
616	Ethelfrith captured Chester, cutting Welsh off frc Britons of the north.

617	Edwin killed Ethelfrith, whose sons Oswald and Oswy fled to Iona for sanctuary. Edwin became king of Northumbria.
627	Edwin and his whole people baptized by bishops Paulinus and Rhun.
633	Edwin killed by Penda of Mercia.
	Oswald returned from Iona, defeated Mercians at battle of Heavenfield. Became king of Northumbria and Bretwalda of England.
635	Bishop Aidan sent from Iona to help Oswald convert his people. Founded Lindisfarne.
642	King Oswald killed by Penda at Oswestry.
c. 650	Prince Peada's conversion and mission to Mercia.
	Creation of Sandbach crosses.
655	King Oswy defeated and killed Penda at River Winwaed.
	Flowering of artistic genius among the English.
670	Erection of the Ruthwell Cross.

Index